The Chakras
and the
Human Energy Fields

THE
CHAKRAS
and the
Human Energy Fields

Shafica Karagulla, M.D.
and
Dora van Gelder Kunz

*This publication made possible with
the assistance of the Kern Foundation*

The Theosophical Publishing House
Wheaton, Ill. U.S.A.
Madras, India/London, England

The Theosophical Publishing House
306 West Geneva Road
Wheaton, IL 60187
A publication of the Theosophical Publishing House, a department
of the Theosophical Society in America.

Library of Congress Cataloging-in-Publication Data

Karagulla, Shafica.
    The chakras and the human energy fields.
    (A Quest book)
    "A Quest original"—T. p. verso.
    Bibliography: p.
    Includes index.
    1. Chakras (Theosophy)   I. Kunz, Dora,
1904-   II. Title.
BP573.C5K37   1989   610   88-40489
ISBN 0-8356-0641-4 (pbk.)
ISBN 0-8356-0650-3 (clth.)

Printed in the United States of America

Second Printing July 1989

Contents

FIVE - THE ROLE OF CONSCIOUSNESS

APPENDIX: Case Histories

Foreword

DORA VAN GELDER KUNZ

My association with Dr. Shafica Karagulla began in New York City shortly after we first met in the 1950s, and most of the clairvoyant investigations we made together took place during the following decade, although we worked intermittently after she moved to California in the 1960s. Dr. Karagulla was primarily interested in research concerning the disease process in relation to the chakras, and therefore most of our cases had this orientation.

During the more than twenty years which have passed since we did this work together, the main focus of my own interest has been therapeutic, and my efforts have been to help people with severe illnesses who are suffering pain. This change in emphasis in my work has been gradual, although it received a greater impetus from the development of a method of healing called "Therapeutic Touch," which Dolores Krieger and I initiated, and which has been taught to thousands of nurses.

During the subsequent years, I have seen hundreds of patients suffering from a wide range of illnesses. Therefore I have learned a great deal more about the disease process than I knew at the time the investigations with Dr. Karagulla took place. In fact, we never really worked together on the therapeutic aspects of our research.

I met Dr. Viola Petitt Neal, who was Shafica Karagulla's teacher and closest friend, but she did not participate in the actual work that we did in New York City. Later, when they were living together in California, I came to know her much better, and to appreciate her deep devotion to spiritual principles. She was very much interested in the book project, and contributed the outline of the basic ideas in the first three chapters.

During my visits to California, Dr. Karagulla talked to me about the possibility of organizing our research material and writing it up for publication in book form. Prior to her death, Dr. Neal participated in many of these conversations. It was always agreed among the three of us that I would have the opportunity to review the manuscript and make whatever changes I thought were required. Dr. Karagulla kept me informed of her progress, and telephoned me about it only a week before her sudden and unexpected death, which was a great shock to all of us.

A few weeks after her fatal accident, the materials upon which the book was to be based came into my hands, as her family agreed that they should be given to me with full rights to oversee publication. I had thought the manuscript at or near completion but was surprised to find that many of the chapters were mere notes. I decided that much more work would need to be done before it was ready for publication, and I therefore asked my friend Emily Sellon, a professional editor, to undertake the task. As a result, the original manuscript as designed by Dr. Karagulla and Dr. Neal has had to be extensively revised, for which I take responsibility. Even the title has been altered, although this was agreed upon before Dr. Karagulla's death.

Under these difficult circumstances, it will be understood that this book contains a mixture of views and contributions. In order to gain coherence, these have been blended together and shaped into final form by Mrs. Sellon.

Shafica Karagulla was a dear friend and a rare individual who combined medical and scientific professionalism with a completely open mind and an eager interest in unexplored fields. During our long friendship her enthusiasm for the possibilities opened up by our investigations never flagged. This book could not have been accomplished without her sustained and thoughtful interest, and our efforts to make it readable and understandable are offered as a tribute to her.

Acknowledgments

Grateful acknowledgment is made to all those who contributed financially to the research on which this book is based: To the Eliot D. Pratt Foundation, which made the initial three-year grant without which the investigations could never have begun; to Trudy Pratt and her late husband, Eliot, for their pioneering spirit in supporting the project. To all who contributed to the Eliot D. Pratt Foundation to support research into higher-sense perception: Rebekah Harkness and the Harkness Foundation; the Lester Finkelstein Foundation, and Irene and the late Lester Finkelstein.

To those who helped support the Higher Sense Perception Research Foundation: The Boston Foundation, Annabelle Markson and the late Yoland Markson; Lynn Charleson for his continuing support; Tom and Gayle den Dass; The Midway Foundation; and the John E. Fetzer Foundation.

To those who gave their time freely for research into their gifts of higher sense perception, especially Frances Farrelly, whose great good humor and common sense lightened the labor of repeated experiments.

To Eloise Doerfler, who has given her time freely for five years in faithfully transcribing the data and ensuring its accuracy; without her patience and support it would have been an impossible task.

To the secretaries for transcribing data, a task that extended over many years: Evelyn Petersen, Helen English, and Maxine Friend.

To Irene Bagge for reading the manuscript and making helpful suggestions.

To the Theosophical Publishing House, for permission to use the color plates and other illustrations from *The Chakras* by C.W. Leadbeater.

Finally, to two close relatives of Shafica Karagulla, Basim Azzam and Fahmi Karagulla, whose generous financial support helped make possible the organization of the research, and insured that personal needs were met, so that she was freed to devote her time to organizing and writing up the case histories.

Introduction

SHAFICA KARAGULLA

> One everlasting whisper, day and night
>   repeated so:
> Something hidden. Go and find it.
> Go and look behind the Ranges,
> Something lost behind the Ranges,
> Lost and waiting for you. Go!
>   Rudyard Kipling, *The Explorer*

Over fifty years ago, my teacher, friend, colleague, and associate in research, Viola Petitt Neal, wrote the above poem in my high school autograph book, and its phrases have echoed in my mind time and time again. But what was hidden that I should find?

As a physician, I was attracted to the working of the human mind, the consciousness of man with its myriad forms of expression. As a neuropsychiatrist, I studied its abnormal expressions in the form of hallucinations, illusions, delusions, and the loss of insight into one's behavior, which included many forms of diseases of the brain resulting in infections, atrophies, or cancer.

The research of Dr. Wilder Penfield on the electrical stimulation of the brain of conscious epileptic patients gave me another range of understanding. All this was prelude to the study of the higher levels of perception which the human mind is capable of. The discovery of some individuals who had broken through the five-sense barrier was the next challenge that forced me to "go and look behind the ranges."

1

How could one verify such abilities for higher perception in those who claimed to possess them? The search to discover that which was "hidden" led me to Mrs. Kunz and other talented people who have helped me to understand part of the mystery that is man. The research on which this book is based stems initially from an effort to show that the information obtained through higher perception has a meaningful and verifiable basis. Later, I began to glimpse the true causes of diseases which give rise to physical and psychic dissonances and reveal the ways in which pain can be relieved and health restored.

From clairvoyants we learn that the personality includes three types of energy fields—the etheric or vital, the astral or emotional, and the mental—all of which surround and interpenetrate every cell of the physical body. The interplay among these three fields may be likened to what a musician calls the major chord, which is composed of three frequencies that in combination with four other notes form an octave of seven frequencies. It is said by some that every human being emits a unique tonal pattern which is created by his individual energy fields working in unison. This is sometimes referred to as the personality note. A perfect tone indicates health, whereas dissonance in the fields and their major centers indicates disease. All this is discussed in subsequent chapters.

This book is an effort to integrate medical science with an investigation of the subtler aspects and energies of human personality, so as to indicate their intricate and close interdependency.

Each of the three persons who contributed to the preparation of the material for this book has her own field of expertise. Dr. Neal is responsible for suggesting the discussion of the constitution of man,[1] based upon theosophical and esoteric concepts; Mrs. Kunz is responsible

---

1. When Dr. Karagulla wrote up her research many years ago, she used the term "man" to mean mankind, which of course includes women. The term and its pronouns are conveniences that we hope do not offend our readers.

for the clairvoyant observations; I myself am responsible for the selection and correlation of the data presented and the medical interpretations.

Dr. Viola Petitt Neal studied physics, chemistry and psychology in college, and obtained her Ph.D. degree in philosophy from London University, her focus being the secret religions of the Middle East. Subsequently she taught what is broadly termed "the Perennial Philosophy" for over thirty-five years, both privately and on college campuses in California. She collaborated with me in writing *Breakthrough to Creativity* though her name does not appear on the cover. In 1978 she published a book of her poems called *Fragments of Experience: A Spiritual Journey*, and in *Through the Curtain* (Neal and Karagulla, 1983) she testified to her awareness of several dimensions of reality and states of consciousness.[2]

Dora van Gelder Kunz was born with exceptional clairvoyant abilities into a family where her mother and grandmother were similarly gifted. In her childhood, her paranormal faculties were developed during her association with the British clairvoyant, Charles W. Leadbeater, the author of such well-known studies as *The Chakras* and *Man Visible and Invisible*. Her ability to perceive and study fairies, angels and other nature spirits in detail has resulted in two works: a monograph about the angelic kingdoms entitled *The Christmas of the Angels*, and *The Real World of Fairies*, a book which gives us a charming and unorthodox picture of the nature spirits which have been part of every cultural tradition.

Mrs. Kunz was the sensitive called "Diane" and "DVG" in my book, *Breakthrough to Creativity*. She is endowed with the gift of perceiving not only the etheric or vital field and its major centers of energy (chakras), but also

2. Because of the untimely death of Dr. Neal in 1981, before the completion of this manuscript, the sections based on her material have been revised by Emily B. Sellon in order to present the esoteric view of the constitution of man more completely, since this forms the indispensable ground upon which the work is based.

the astral (emotional) and mental fields with their corresponding centers. This natural faculty has been developed to a high degree of accuracy through her patient efforts at careful and detailed observation, trained interpretation, and correlation with medical case histories. She has worked with other physicians in diagnosing difficult or ambiguous medical cases, and in recent years has specialized in the teaching and practice of a method of healing known as "Therapeutic Touch," which she developed with her colleague, Dr. Dolores Krieger.

From 1975 to 1987, Mrs. Kunz was President of The Theosophical Society in America and editor of its journal, *The American Theosophist*; since leaving that office she has devoted most of her time to her healing work. Because of her ability to perceive both the causes of illness and the efficacy of the healing process, she adds a valuable dimension to our understanding of the mechanism of health and disease.

I myself am a physician, and neuropsychiatry is my specialty. After training in psychiatry at the University of Edinburgh under Sir David K. Henderson, my subsequent research required an extensive perusal of mental case histories involving various types of hallucinations, such as the hearing of voices, the seeing of visions, and the experiencing of abnormal sensations. In some cases these were definitely related to brain damage, such as general paralysis in the insane, Alzheimer's disease, or toxic conditions as in bromine intoxication.

In the meantime, the work of Dr. Wilder Penfield of the Montreal Neurological Institute in Canada drew my attention. His book, *The Cerebral Cortex of Man*, described the inducing of hallucinations and other abnormal experiences in epileptic patients who were undergoing surgical operations of the brain in full waking consciousness. Attracted by his work in mapping out the different functions of the cerebral cortex, I went to Canada and was fortunate in having the opportunity of working with Dr. Penfield for more than three and a half years. Some of the research I did at that time was published in a paper in the *British Medical Journal* in 1955, entitled "Psychical Phenomena in Temporal Lobe Epilepsy and the Psychoses" (Karagulla and Robertson). In it, we pointed out the similarity of the hallucinatory experiences between psychical phenomena in temporal lobe epilepsy and in schizophrenia.

Shortly thereafter, I was invited to enter the United States to continue my research in schizophrenia, and was appointed assistant professor in psychiatry at the University of New York. Still seeking a solution to the different types of hallucinations in mental patients, I was challenged to read some unorthodox books about the human mind and its potential which my neuropsychiatric training had not included.

Thus before venturing into this new field, I had done over twelve years of research into the human mind, both sane and insane, and my neuropsychiatric training was entirely of the usual academic and scientific variety. My interests, however, were less orthodox. All the material I was reading seemed to suggest a vastly more complex view of the nature of man, transcending the limitations of the physical brain and the five physical senses, and challenging conservative medical concepts.

So I began to investigate for myself. Part of the research I did at that time in the field of the paranormal was published in 1967 in *Breakthrough to Creativity*, which presented documented evidence about the higher octaves of our sense perception. The need, as I saw it, was to discover and analyze the mechanisms governing these higher dimensions of perception. How do they arise, and how do they function? There is nothing "supernatural" in the universe; whatever phenomena appear so to us are the result of our ignorance of the laws that govern them.

The publication of this book elicited many letters from physicians, scientists and others with similar experiences, and this led me to further research with the help of gifted individuals like Mrs. Kunz. As a result, I began to understand, at least in part, the mechanism of these abilities.

This and other research points significantly to the fact

that in addition to the electrical and magnetic fields which surround all physical events there are other types of energies and frequencies that are as yet undetectable by any instrumentation so far developed. For this reason, the gifted human being is the only "instrument" so far available for the kind of research which correlates clairvoyant perceptions with medical diagnoses. In the case of Mrs. Kunz, I demanded as much detail as possible concerning her observations.

In our work together, I served as the researcher and she as the observer. Our method began by presenting her with average, healthy subjects, so that I could learn how and what she perceived. After a year, I was able to develop an outline of the various characteristics to be looked for in studying the state of health or disease; thereafter we followed these guidelines consistently in every case.

We studied first the general characteristics of the etheric or vital body, its relationship to the vortices of energy, or chakras, within the field, the effects of these on the endocrine glands, and how they related to other centers. Later we to some extent observed the emotional and the mental fields with their corresponding vortices of energy, but more research is needed in those aspects of the human complex.

The outpatient clinic for endocrine diseases of one of New York's most prestigious medical centers was the major source of our medical data. Mrs. Kunz never spoke to any of the patients. She only perceived them at a distance of a few meters while she was sitting in the back of the outpatient waiting room.

It is worth noting that Mrs. Kunz had been accustomed to seeing physically healthy or emotionally disturbed people; here she was for the first time systematically observing the etheric field and chakras in severely ill patients, some of whom had had removal of parts of the body or the glands. We found that abnormalities observed in the major etheric chakras were an indication of a tendency to a disease process, and that the area in which this would occur could be predicted even years before the symptoms began to manifest.

As our studies progressed, we learned that what may appear to originate in one dimension, as, for example, at the etheric level, may actually derive from a deeper level such as the emotional or mental. Abnormalities and tumors of the thyroid gland may appear to originate at the etheric throat center, yet further observation may point to the cause as being in the emotions, just as physical diseases seem to originate at the etheric level.

We will offer case histories to illustrate this point, and to substantiate our theory that the human being is a complex network of interconnected processes that are fed by energies arising from three or more universal fields, all of which play a vital role in health and disease.

The main objects of Parts One, Two and Three of this book are to present some historical context for clairvoyant research, as well as a brief outline of the constitution of man as conceived in the esoteric tradition. Part Four presents research into those aspects of the human personality wherein clairvoyant observation perceives health as a state of harmony and disease as a state of dissonance, correlated with medical evidence regarding the physical state of the subjects, and Part Five considers the importance of consciousness as a factor in both health and disease, as well as in personal change and growth, with a final note on where such investigations as these may take us in the future.

1

A New View of
Human Nature

I
The Dawn of a
New Consciousness

Today the winds of change are gusting through our world, blowing away many old prejudices, unsettling the stability of institutions and the endurance of "truths" long taken for granted. There is every sign that we are at the dawn of a new era of human discovery and accomplishment. Many people are dismayed at the rate of change, fearful that we will be unable to control the unprecedented discoveries and techniques which are opening up new areas of knowledge about nature; others welcome the challenge. But all recognize that our world-picture will change dramatically in the coming decades.

We are breaking through the frontiers of space above and beyond our planet, and are probing the minute inner spaces of physical matter. Both of these achievements move us multidimensionally into new levels of space-time with energies hitherto unrecognized. It has become a commonplace if terrifying fact of twentieth-century life that the old scientific picture of a solid material world has vanished in favor of a universe that is charged with stupendous energies. In the years since the first splitting of the atom, we have discovered that the organization and behavior of the atomic realm are stable and enduring, thus giving the world an appearance of solid form, but that the energies within this realm are moving at incredible rates of speed. This new understanding of the universe as a stable pattern within which tremendous charges of energy move in and out demands a change in our world-view—a wholly different concept of reality from that which grew out of nineteenth-century materialist science.

Hitherto, we humans have pursued our games of war and peace in the confident belief that we could control change and enhance the quality of life merely by manipulating our environment: applied technology would create a perfect society. But we have found to our sorrow that it is the seemingly uncontrollable human factors which dominate the world scene. We are also beginning to realize that it is the subtler aspects of life—unpredictable, hard to identify, impossible to measure—that govern human behavior. And going beyond the purely human sphere to that all-encompassing nature of which we are a part, we now understand that life is a very complex relationship between the individual and its environment, and that this environment is not limited, but includes the Earth and indeed the whole universe.

This growing perception of the interrelatedness of all living things has many implications. For our purposes, however, we focus on the fact that there is a continuous energy exchange between the individual and the environment which every living system (whether human, animal, vegetable, or even chemical) regulates in terms of its own self-organization. This energy exchange is so constant and so indispensable for all living organisms that it can be regarded as a universal field effect. We discuss this at some length in the section on *The Fields and the Chakras*. But here we note particularly that self-regulation throughout nature is achieved from within, not imposed from without, and that this implies a degree of conscious control, even if consciousness in this context is very different from what we experience at the human level. Erich Jantsch wrote in *The Self-Organizing Universe*, "If consciousness is defined as the degree of autonomy a system gains in the dynamic relations with its environment, even the simplest . . . systems such as chemical dissipative structures have a primitive form of *consciousness*" (p. 40). The all-pervading role of consciousness at every level of organization is a postulate important in the work reported in this book.

The implications of this emerging paradigm are yet to be measured. What life is, and what it means to be a whole, functioning, healthy living organism, is now perceived as a multidimensional process, involving a delicate and dynamic balance of many energy systems and levels of integration. To this list we add: many levels of consciousness, even within the physical organism itself, for each of these systems "knows" its own function. These subtler levels of existence, moreover, are universal (at least so far as this earth is concerned), for the energies involved are as much a part of existence as the forces of gravity or electromagnetism. No living particle can escape them. Thus we are already moving beyond a purely mechanical interpretation of life.

The notion of fields is introduced to every school child who is exposed to the experiment of proving that when electricity flows through a wire it establishes a magnetic field. Other physical field phenomena can also be easily demonstrated, although detection of the nuclear fields requires more sophisticated equipment. But when we posit a universal life or vital field (as we do in this book), this is much more difficult to demonstrate in a tangible way, for there are as yet no scientific instruments capable of detecting the presence of such a field. Yet "life," if as yet undefined, is real, and the living (as open systems) have specific characteristics not shared by inorganic matter. The most important of these is the ability to replenish energy (what we call vitality) without an outside agency, which no machine can do.

The concept that the earth is embedded in a series of universal fields is here broadened to include not only the life energy (whose effects upon such physical processes as the immune system have not as yet been possible to measure), but also mind and emotion, which we accept as universal concomitants of life. All living creatures exhibit choice (likes and dislikes) as well as volition; life is a learning process, and evolution implies a growth in assimilated knowledge.

This process is enormously accelerated in human beings. But in us the assimilation of knowledge becomes more critical, for it involves the uses to which that knowledge is put. Self-understanding and an appreciation of the higher possibilities of the human spirit have become imperative for our very survival.

In the new view of human life which is just emerging, man's inner resources are seen to embody not only his physical systems but also a process for replenishing vitality, and an almost untapped resource of higher energies which can harmonize and integrate the mind and emotions with the physical body, thus enhancing all of life.

What are some of the implications?

As human beings become more and more aware that the body is a vehicle which the self uses for its own purposes (whether good or bad, constructive or destructive), this developing self-awareness produces tides of restlessness, such as those which are sweeping over peoples and nations today. Freedom for self-expression is the criterion of modern life. Although some of the results of this phenomenon are negative, even destructive, it signals that the awakening self in man is seeking to explore more complex aspects of his own nature, as well as wider ranges of experience.

Certain aspects of this new development—such as the ethics of recent medical and biochemical discoveries— have become controversial; others, especially those which deal with the higher energy fields, are not generally accepted. All of these hold out great promise for increased human understanding, but they also hold some dangers. The whole area is a new world of exploration without many signposts for guidance or criteria of credibility. Therefore, knowledge is essential, lest we be led astray into irrational beliefs, or accept dubious conclusions on insufficient evidence.

What is needed, from our point of view, is a careful

study of the postulate that man is an intelligent, conscious self, functioning simultaneously on several levels of complexity—physical, vital, emotional, and mental—and interacting constantly with the universal energies of nature itself. Beyond these, there is the much deeper level of true selfhood: the soul, with all its characteristics of intentionality, integration, creativity, compassion, insight and, ultimately, spiritual awareness.

This doctrine is far from new, for it has been part of the esoteric tradition, both East and West, for numberless generations. What is new is the effort to map onto this esoteric view of man the enormous gains in contemporary knowledge, in order to develop a true science of the self. If successful, this effort can give us the perspective, the tools and the impetus to make a quantum jump in our understanding of human nature and the range of human possibility.

II
Breaking the Barrier
of the Senses

Throughout the long evolutionary journey of life on this planet, living forms have developed within the narrow constraints set by nature. Like the caterpillar wrapped in its cocoon, man's experience has been limited to the range of his five senses. The conscious perceiver and interpreter of his physical environment, he has been largely unaware of the presence of other dimensions of reality which lay all about him. This is particularly true of modern man.

But today we recognize that the sensed world is far from being the only "real" domain of experience, and that in fact our senses merely deliver impressions to us that the mind/brain interprets according to its own inner vision. Moreover, the narrow boundaries of the sensed world are crumbling, as our knowledge expands to include quantum reality as well as the information bombarding us from outer space. The possibility of extending our understanding into realms long hidden from us by the limitations of the senses is opening an ever vaster world to us—a world which, far from being remote, is now seen to lie all around us, and even to be part of our own being.

As we seek to explore the world of finer perceptions, a number of questions arise. What are the mechanisms for perceiving the hidden world which lies beyond the reach of our senses? Can we develop the capacity and use it creatively and constructively?

At this stage of inquiry we are very much in the position of the blind men in the parable, each of whom tried to describe an elephant in terms of that portion of the animal he was able to grasp. Similarly, in a village of a hundred inhabitants, if ninety-eight were color-blind we could expect them to be very skeptical of the descriptions of the remaining two people who perceived the full spectrum of prismatic colors. In fact, they probably would be sure that these two were visionaries, or story-telling, or just hallucinating. However, if over a period of time 20 percent of the inhabitants began to see the whole spectrum, the rest might begin to concede the possibility that it might exist, even though beyond their own perception. This story is somewhat analogous to the present state of affairs vis-à-vis extrasensory perception.

There are many signs that the next great adventure for humanity will take place in the realm of consciousness, and that a whole range of yet unexplored possibilities awaits us. These raise many unanswered questions. What are the boundaries of the self? Where do self and environment begin and end? Can we develop reliable mechanisms for discovering these subtle interrelationships?

Just as the five physical senses give us access to a certain range of physical reality, so the higher senses allow us to perceive elements of the supersensory world. Higher sense perception includes clairvoyance, which means "clear seeing," and usually refers to the ability to perceive the vital and/or the emotional field. Because such perceptions have seemed to be both exotic and idiosyncratic (since they are experienced by the few), today's scientists and researchers have never tried in any systematic way to explore and understand the mechanisms which permit such phenomena to exist. In a culture committed to the scientific method, this neglect would appear to stem from a fundamental prejudice or misconception.

Scientists have held that it lies outside the province of their discipline to investigate claims that it is possible to perceive states of matter subtler than the physical. For this reason, the painstaking work of J.B. Rhine in the field of telepathy and clairvoyance had little impact upon the scientific community. But physicists concerned with quantum physical reality are investigating probabilities and indeterminacies which are far removed from the so-called facts of our gross physical world, and can only be "observed" through their effects. Is it not also likely that if we were to extend our explorations into the subtler aspects of that world, we might find these dimensions just as lawful, just as amenable to study and understanding as the complex and ambiguous world of quantum reality?

Nevertheless, some research is going forward in this area, using man himself as the sensor, such as the practice of healing methods like Therapeutic Touch. Sensitives who can observe the interactions of vitality, emotion and thought processes remove these interactions from the realm of the purely subjective. Their observations, however, differ in degree, in clarity and in comprehension. Some of them perceive only the etheric or life field; others perceive both the field and the etheric centers (chakras) which are a key element in the basic pattern that characterizes man, both as an individual personality and as a member of the human species. Some clairvoyants see the astral or emotional field, rather than the etheric. Such psychics do not usually perceive the chakras within the emotional field unless they have been trained to do so, or have great natural gifts. The mental field and its centers are seen only by those with a highly developed type of specialized clairvoyance.

Thus far, breakthroughs into these levels of reality have met with a great deal of confusion and misunderstanding. The result has been a flood of "psychic" literature of very uneven quality and credibility, all claiming to furnish accurate information about the supersensory dimensions of human experience. Unfortunately many people, bored and dissatisfied with the present-day scene and its lack of values, accept these accounts uncritically. Such enthusiasts often plunge into personal experimentation without regard for the pitfalls that could be encountered in entering any new area of experience without previous knowledge or preparation. Like the ability to walk or fly, such capacities must be developed. This takes time, patience and much more effort than those who are eager for new sensations wish to expend. Thus interest in the so-called psychic world often becomes more of an escape from the constraints of every-day life than a serious search for new knowledge.

This situation does not change the fact that many people today are exhibiting various degrees of paranormal ability, including clairvoyance, clairaudience, precognition, telepathy, psychometry, dowsing, and healing. It is beginning to look as though these abilities are emergent, and may eventually become a normal part of human consciousness. If we accept the concept mentioned before, that evolution is a learning process, we realize that living systems are continually developing new capacities for a creative response to their environment. If this is so, why should not human beings begin to extend their perception to supersensory levels, and develop the ability to explore more encompassing dimensions of reality?

The first requirement for the development of higher sense perception is a recognition that the supersensory realms are not opened up "magically," but are regulated by natural laws just as precise as those which govern the physical world. If they are to become known to us, we must define more precisely the ranges of supersensory perception; the energies involved and their relationship to physical health and disease; the effects of behavior; the role of the mind and of mental images, intent, and motivation; and much more. Since there are different types of extrasensory perception, and since all observation is filtered through the percipient's mind, we must also determine the degree of "observer effect" in clairvoyant investigation, and develop a system of checks and balances, as well as a common vocabulary. These are only a few of the requirements if we are to bring more order and coherence into the whole field, especially as it bears upon our understanding of the human being.

So far, medicine has been concerned with problems of the physical organism, achieving very important results, even though the question of how healing takes place still remains a mystery. Today our ability to deal with hitherto intractable diseases has been enormously enhanced through the development of scientific sensors, which allow the body to be seen from a number of different aspects. Infrared and liquid crystals give a heat color pattern called thermography; the newest medical instrumentation using ultrasound and nuclear magnetic resonance gives us other dimensions and patterns. At a more fundamental level of physical being, we are becoming accustomed to thinking of ourselves in terms of systems, processes, and patterns of energy, rather than of dense materiality.

Sensitives who can observe the interactions of vital energy with emotional and mental processes could remove these interactions from the realm of the purely subjective by acting as human "sensors." The observations of those gifted with such abilities, however, differ widely as to the reliability of their faculty, as well as in its clarity, precision, and applicability to physical situations. In spite of these problems, we must persist, since the field holds so much promise.

Perhaps the most important conclusion that emerges from a study of the extensions of physical perception, which clairvoyance makes possible, is that the physical brain is not the originator of consciousness, but rather its instrument. Acceptance of this concept would have far-reaching effects upon the way we humans look at ourselves, and thus upon the world we live in.

Up to this point in human evolution, the world of the five senses has been our safe and familiar environment, a school for learning which has seemed to set the boundaries of human experience. Unaware of the possibility of experiencing a world beyond the physical, we have only caught glimpses of its dimensions through the arts or through the witness of mystics, saints, and seers. But now science has also begun to probe some aspects of this vaster world. More and more exotic discoveries are being made and startling theories propounded about the nature of our universe. Since it now seems that a considerable number of people have experienced some portions of the super-sensory realm for themselves, should we not make every effort to bring these experiences under serious scrutiny?

It is our hope that the material offered in this book will be helpful in suggesting some of the principles that govern the subtler dimensions of our world—dimensions we all share in equally, if unknowingly. They are part of that greater whole which comprehends not only the physical earth with all its past history and future possibilities, but also the thoughts and feelings, errors and accomplishments, insights and intuitions of all its inhabitants.

2

The Fields and the Chakras

III
The Three Fields of the Personal Self

We begin with an exploration of a further question: What is the nature of our supersensory environment, and how does it affect us?

As noted in Chapter I, our thesis is that man is a complex of interacting processes, all of which are indispensable. No physical experience is unaccompanied by emotional response and mental interpretation. If we try to codify the levels of human experience, we arrive at a schema which is close to the theosophical view that man expresses himself in physical life through a threefold mechanism: the *etheric* or vital, the *astral* or emotional, and the *mental*, all of which, taken together, are referred to in theosophical literature as the personality.

We know full well that this description of the human psyche is remote from that offered by current schools of psychology, but it is nevertheless the hypothesis upon which our research is based.

When these three aspects of human nature are integrated with the physical body into a harmonious whole, this becomes a complete and flexible instrument for the expression of the self. The word "self," in turn, is reserved for the deepest and most enduring essence of that which each of us really is—our true being.

The personality is much like the notion of persona as it

was developed in ancient Greece and Rome: a mask or appearance which the actor dons to indicate the role he is playing in the drama. In the drama of life, we, the actors, usually become so identified with this representation that we mistake it for the real self. It is no exaggeration to say that one of the greatest struggles for human beings is to become aware of the difference between the self (which some call the soul) and its persona or personality.

Another important element of this view of human nature is related to the mystery of life and of life energies. We are now quite familiar with the concept of the physical body as a hierarchy of interacting systems of organization, but the additional idea that these systems are characterized by specific energy patterns is as yet little understood. But it is with these energy patterns that our research is concerned, and therefore we need a principle which can explain the correspondences between the energy patterns and the physical symptoms.

In the view being developed here, man is a system of interdependent force fields, within which energy patterns are not only appropriate to the particular field but are also ordered by special processes and mechanisms. Furthermore, these energy patterns are responsive to changes in consciousness, a fact which gives us a very different perspective upon many of the troubling problems of human life. In esoteric literature, man is described as having seven levels or fields of consciousness and energy, each of which is hierarchically differentiated in a way somewhat analogous to the solid, liquid, gaseous, molecular, atomic and subatomic subdivisions of the physical world.

We have already noted that our study is principally concerned with the etheric field, which is in constant interaction with the physical body. But since there can be no separation between physical and psychological processes, there are many instances in which emotional and mental factors must be taken into consideration.

Thus we have adopted the theosophical description of human nature as our working hypothesis, in terms of which we have evaluated the clairvoyant observations that form the body of our research. And here we might define our use of the word *hypothesis* as "a proposition which we will assume to be true in order to test certain facts against it." If the hypothesis provides a meaningful explanatory principle it will be reinforced by our research; if not, it can be modified in favor of a better hypothesis.

As we shall constantly be talking about fields, we must emphasize once more that we are only justified in referring to the life energies, feelings, and thoughts associated with every individual as "fields" if we hold them to be special instances or intensifications of *universal* fields in which all life participates. (A field may be generally defined as a continuous condition of space.) In this case, there is a constant interaction not only among the three fields associated with each individual, but also between these and the universal fields of which they are a part.

In order to avoid confusion, therefore, in general descriptions we shall usually employ the term "field" to refer to the universal aspect, and reserve the words "vehicle" or "body" to identify the individual expression of the universal field. But because DVK (Dora van Gelder Kunz) is so accustomed to speaking about fields rather than bodies, in many of the case histories to follow the term "general field" will appear in descriptions of the etheric or astral body, as distinguished from the energy flow through the chakra system.

The interweaving of the three fields of the personal self, together with their vehicle, the physical body, gives us a picture of human life which can be compared to a moving four-dimensional tapestry, whose warp and woof are composed of threads of differing qualities and textures, and whose patterns shift and change as they cut across the path of time. The key to understanding the complexity of this process of interaction lies in its dynamism, for life is always characterized by growth and change. The important factor in such change is whether it is taking us in the direction of negativity, ill health, and disease, and whether this pattern can be altered in the direction of self-integration, health, and wholeness.

IV

The Structure and Function of the Etheric Body

The most important function of the etheric body is the transfer of life energy or vitality from the universal field to the individual field, and thence to the physical body. It is the primary contact with the ocean of life energy that sustains all of nature. Vitality per se is not recognized as a form of energy in the West, but in the East, where it is known as *prana*, it has always been perceived as a universal force in nature connected with breathing and breath. It is active in plants and animals as well as humans.

The etheric also acts as a connecting link between the physical body and the emotional and mental vehicles, although all of these are interpenetrating and synchronized, thus constituting, with the physical body, the instrument of the conscious self during the whole of life.

At the etheric level, the individual field is conditioned and vitalized by the life force or etheric energy which pours in through its major centers or chakras, which are described in detail later. At the same time, the centers at the emotional and mental levels are processing energies from these fields, and these energies condition and modify the etheric energy as it flows through the network of channels in the etheric body. It is thus a very complex process. The etheric body vitalizes the physical body, but exactly how this takes place is not yet known. Since the etheric channels run parallel to the nervous system, however, there may be a process of induction.

Much as the unborn child floats in the embryonic fluid of the womb, so human beings are sustained by a sea of nourishing energies. The structure of the centers of force or chakras in the etheric, astral and mental vehicles remains constant throughout the lifetime of the individual, even while they are being continually replenished by the energies moving in and out from the three corresponding fields.

Every physical particle has its etheric counterpart (hence the term "etheric double") which is a perfect replica of the physical form. The etheric vehicle is so closely interwoven with the physical body that the two are inseparable. In one sense, certainly, the etheric *is* physical, in that it is never separated from the body during life and disintegrates with it at death. For that reason the etheric has historically been described in esoteric literature as the fourth state of matter, taking the solid, liquid and gaseous states as the first three. It should be remarked, however, that observers have reported that liquids and gases as well as solids have their etheric counterparts, and therefore this categorization seems weak.

In fact, the etheric field is said to be subdivided into several categories, the densest of which is associated with physical solids, while others are more rarefied. The etheric is in fact "material," and it lies very close to physical matter. For this reason, it has been suggested that the ability to see the etheric field vaguely is related to the retina of the eye, and just on the threshold of ordinary vision. If this is the case, it might be possible to devise some kind of instrumentation capable of enhancing the etheric field to the point of visibility. Many have tried to do this, but so far without success.

The etheric is not only the vehicle of the life force or prana; it also furnishes the basic pattern according to which the physical body is built. (The connections between the etheric pattern and the genetic code offer interesting possibilities which have so far not been explored.) This etheric matrix is important since it is directly related to the individual's state of health, for the quality, sensitivity and resilience of the physical body are directly related to the tone and quality of the etheric body.

Every cell in the human body has its equivalent etheric, emotional and mental energies localized around it. The energies which are localized around each individual (constituting the "bodies" or "aura") attenuate into space or, to put it more accurately, into the universal fields. Much more work needs to be done in order to clarify how the three fields relate to one another in an individual; so far, as mentioned before, we have had to limit our studies chiefly to the etheric, with only brief forays into the emotional and mental fields for diagnostic purposes. Thus all that has so far been possible is to sketch the gross anatomy of the etheric body with its chakras.

To the clairvoyant, the etheric body looks like a luminous web of fine bright lines of force which, in a healthy person, stand out at right angles to the surface of the skin. Its texture may be fine-grained or coarse, a characteristic which repeats itself in the physical body type. Each organ of the body has its etheric counterpart, through which the etheric energy circulates constantly.

The color of the etheric body is a pale blue-gray or violet-gray, slightly luminous and shimmering, like heat waves above the earth on hot days. In the average person it extends from five to seven centimeters (two to three inches) beyond the periphery of the physical body, gradually fading away into the enveloping ocean of etheric energy. This ocean of energy is in constant rapid motion, and surrounds the body much as the atmosphere surrounds the earth.

While the etheric is not in itself a vehicle of consciousness, it does transmit the stream of consciousness to the physical brain, and if it is separated for any reason from the physical body, the result is disturbance and ill health.

There is an etheric web of the finest texture that acts as a natural barrier between the etheric and astral fields, and protects the individual from opening communication between these two levels prematurely. Some theosophical literature, especially the works of C.W. Leadbeater, describes this web as closely knit, composed of a single layer of etheric atoms separating the chakras as they lie along the spine. It is in effect a protective device, and its injury has serious consequences, since this opens the door to forces beyond the individual's control. Among the factors reported to modify or tear this web are alcoholism and the continued use of narcotics and similar substances.

It should not be supposed, however, that the existence of this etheric web inhibits the normal interaction between the emotional and etheric fields. In a healthy individual, there is an ordered relationship and a rhythmic flow among all the energy fields. But when there are chronic disturbances on the emotional level, such as continuous hostility or anxiety, the energy discharge is disordered, and this can eventually damage the whole system. To take another example, fear and depression tend to cut down the normal flow of energy, so that organs like the kidneys become less able to function normally. Thus the emotions closely affect both the etheric and physical bodies.

Just as too little energy is damaging, so also is the effect of too much. If the energy flow is too rapid, it can be used up quickly, resulting in a depletion of the body's reservoir of energy. Tension will also deplete energy reserves, and this can have sudden effects at the physical level, such as a heart attack or kidney failure. Energy depletion of this kind has such a pervasive effect that it is not possible to tell where it will manifest or which vital organ will be affected, although DVK is able to see where the depletion is occurring.

When a healthy person is in a calm and happy state of mind, the energy flows evenly and smoothly. The chakras are able to transform energy from level to level in health as well as in disease, so that when an individual is full of affection this is transmitted to the body in the form of increased balanced energy. If there is no emotional conflict, the etheric energy is strengthened and enhanced.

Certainly, healthy children are naturally happy and spontaneous, and they are overflowing with energy. (A more detailed account of the effect of changes in the emotional field will be found in Chapter VI.)

In sum, positive emotions are more economical for the whole system—a fact which scarcely needs emphasis, since everyone knows it more or less instinctively. Certainly our research supports the aims of many techniques being developed today, whose purpose is to inculcate harmonious inner attitudes and so achieve a state of good health and positive personal relationships.

V
The Role of
the Chakras

The chakras are superphysical centers or organs through which the energies of the different fields are synchronized and distributed to the physical body. They are more or less active on the astral, mental and (to some extent) on even higher levels, in which they have different roles, but they are of primary importance at the etheric level, where they serve as instruments for the focusing of energy in the body.

The anatomy of the chakras has been described in Indian and Tibetan tantric literature, and also in the works of C.W. Leadbeater and other modern investigators, such as Swami Rama and Hiroshi Motoyama. DVK has made a detailed and extended study of their features over a long period of time, with special attention to their role in health and disease. The descriptions given here are entirely based on her observations, and will be found to differ in many details from other accounts, although not in essence.

The etheric, astral and mental vehicles each contain seven major centers of force, which have been called chakras because of their shape. In both form and mode of motion they resemble a wheel, with the central core acting as the hub, around which petal-like structures revolve. Through this core the energies of the different fields focus and circulate, and around it the energies whirl

33

centrifugally and pulsate rhythmically, so that the whole looks like a flower whose petals are in constant harmonic motion, somewhat like the effects achieved in time-lapse photography. In fact, in Indian literature the chakras have been referred to as lotuses because of their flower-like form, and because they have a central root or stem which connects them energetically to the spine and nervous system. The cores or hearts of the centers are points of interaction where energy flows from one field or level into another. These are also associated with specific abilities or powers of consciousness related to one or another of the other fields, such as the emotional or mental.

Lama Govinda, well-known exponent of Buddhist Tantrism, has pointed out that the physiological foundations of the doctrine of the chakras or psychic centers is the same in Hindu and Buddhist Tantrism, though there are considerable variations in the two systems. "The main difference," he writes, "lies in the different treatment of the same fundamental facts. . . . The Hindu system emphasizes more the static side of the centers and their connexions with elementary nature. . . . This supplies the chakras with an 'objective' content in the form of permanently fixed seed-syllables. . . . The Buddhist system is less concerned with the static-objective side of the chakras, but rather with that which flows through them, with their dynamic functions, i.e., with the transformation of that current of cosmic or nature-energies into spiritual potentialities."[1] The view of the chakras which DVK presents is akin to the dynamism of the Buddhist system.

The seven etheric chakras, which are so influential in the health of the physical and etheric bodies, have their counterparts on the astral and mental levels. Like the physical body, which is continually disintegrating and rebuilding itself, the etheric, emotional and mental fields are constantly changing, but at a much more rapid rate. The chakras are involved in this change.

---

1. Lama Anagarika Govinda. *Foundations of Tibetan Mysticism*. New York: E.P. Dutton, 1960, p. 134.

It is important to note that the chakras are both the transmitters and the transformers of energy from field to field, for their mechanism synchronizes the emotional, mental and the etheric energies. They step the energy up or down, or slow or speed it up, from one field to another, so that the faster energy of the emotional field can affect the slower energy of the etheric, as well as the reverse.

The etheric chakras are most easily visualized as rapidly spinning vortices, which draw in energy at their cores in a tight flow and disperse it along the periphery of their petals in ever-widening spirals. The torrent of incoming energy from the general field pours into the chakras, and because of their pattern of organization, this produces a whirling or spinning motion. This flow does not affect their basic geometrical structure, however, for that remains constant.

Yet it must not be inferred that the chakras are separate from the fields themselves, as might be implied by the way they appear in the diagrams. They are vortices which concentrate the energy within the fields, just as whirlpools are formations in and of water. Therefore any important change in the energy field is immediately apparent in the chakras, and most easily observed there.

If, for example, a person is emotionally upset over a period of time, this energy goes through the whole of the etheric field as well as the emotional field, and therefore it reacts upon the body's organs such as the kidneys. Conversely, when the body is under stress, some of the outward flow from the etheric through the chakras in turn affects the emotional field.

The colors, which vary from chakra to chakra, also glow in a way that contributes to their flower-like appe rance. In a healthy person, the chakras' forms are beautifully balanced, symmetrical and organic, with all the parts flowing together in a rhythmic pattern. Their motion is, in fact, harmonic or musical in character, with rhythms which vary according to individual, constitutional and temperamental differences.

The centers are never static; their speed of rotation is

both rapid and variable according to the state of health and the quality of the flow. The whole process is analogous to the mechanism of respiration, for the energy is, as it were, breathed in and breathed out by the living human being. The energy pours in through the core of the chakra, reaches the spine via its stalk, then flows along the tiny pathways of the etheric body which are connected with the physical nervous system. It finally returns to the chakras, moving outward in spirals through the periphery of the petals, in a constant intake and outflow. These spirals of energy become wider and wider during the circulation process, gradually blending and fading into the whole field of the etheric body, and then dispersing into the universal field, just as our expelled breath becomes part of the whole atmosphere of the earth.

The etheric chakras, which lie on the surface of the etheric body, vary greatly in shade, brightness, size, rapidity of motion, rhythm and texture, some being finer, some coarser, depending upon individual idiosyncrasy and state of health. For this reason, the disease process is very apparent in the chakras, since it both disrupts their harmonic motion and changes the texture of their material.

The chakras also reveal a person's quality of consciousness and degree of personal development and abilities, through the variations in the etheric centers and their interconnections with those at other levels. In a simple, rather undeveloped person, the chakras will be small in size, slow in movement, dull in color and coarse in texture. In a more intelligent, responsive and sensitive person they will be brighter, of finer texture and with a more rapid movement, and in an awakened individual who makes full use of his powers, they become coruscating whirlpools of color and light.

The major chakras of the etheric body are aligned along a vertical axis, the lower five lying parallel to the spinal cord, extending from the base of the spine to the skull, while the other two are located between the eyebrows and at the top of the head. (See pullout inside back cover.) This latter, the crown chakra, is usually larger than the others, and is the dominant seat of consciousness.

In any one individual, some chakras may vary in size and brilliance, and this, together with the activity of their interconnections, indicates special talents and abilities. For example, the throat and brow centers of a talented singer or speaker will be much larger than the norm, as well as being brighter, more luminous and more rapidly spinning. In a quite different case the solar plexus center of a trance-medium will be enlarged but of a coarser texture, with dark colors and some dysrhythmia and loose- ness in the core. In a newborn baby, the chakras are usually about three centimeters in size and look like hard little disks.

Each of the centers has special links with certain organs of the body, as well as with certain states of consciousness (described later). However, as Arthur Avalon pointed out in his classic on kundalini called *The Serpent Fire*, it should be remembered that although correlations are appropriate, definite identification of the chakras with particular physical organs can be misleading, for the chakras are subtle vital energy centers, which exist while the body is alive and disappear at death; thus they are material, but not physical in the ordinary sense of the word.

With this caveat in mind, we can say that in general our studies have shown that the endocrine glands are related to the seven etheric chakras (see pullout). Certainly the intricate relationships among these chakras, as well as those on other levels, bear a close resemblance to the functional interconnectedness of the endocrine system. In fact, the interaction of all the fields with the physical body is a beautifully integrated system which originates in and is sustained by the energy patterns of the chakras in the etheric, astral and mental vehicles.

The various chakras also indicate the primary emphasis in an individual—the focus of the "I." For example, if a person identifies principally with feelings, the solar plexus and heart center will be more active and prominent than the others. If the brow center is very bright, this indicates a degree of personal integration; if the crown center is especially luminous, it signifies the development of spiritual awareness. The level of activity of the etheric chakras and the degree of sensitivity of their interconnections with their emotional and mental counterparts determine an individual's potential for the development of higher sense perception.

The thread of waking consciousness is connected with the core of the crown chakra. During sleep, this flow of energy diminishes, to be reactivated at the moment of awakening. The life thread, however, connects the heart chakra to the physical heart, and this connection is unbroken throughout life. At the time of death, the thread of consciousness withdraws from the crown center, and the thread of life withdraws from the heart, signalling the disintegration of all the other chakras. Thus at death all the interconnections are broken; the etheric body is first loosened from the physical body, then separates, and disintegrates within a few days after death under normal conditions.

To sum up, the principal functions of the etheric chakras are to absorb and distribute prana or vital energy to the etheric body and, through it, to the physical body, and to maintain dynamic connections with the corresponding chakras in the emotional and mental bodies. One of the functions of the chakras is to coordinate the interaction among the various fields. The condition of the physical body is affected not only by the rate of etheric energy flow, but also by the degree of harmony in its rhythm, and any obstructions which deform the normal energy patterns result in loss of vitality and ill health.

We shall now describe the principal chakras as they are perceived by DVK. The illustrations which we offer for reference on the pullout inside the back cover of this book are from *The Chakras*, a clairvoyant study by C.W. Leadbeater (Wheaton, IL: Theosophical Publishing House, [1927] 1987). Painted from Leadbeater's descriptions, these illustrations of the chakras at the emotional level represent their structure and colors as well as possible in such a static medium, but unfortunately they totally fail to convey the dynamism of the centers and their constantly changing colors and rhythms.

The Crown Chakra

The topmost chakra is located about six centimeters above the crown of the head. Saucerlike in shape, it consists of 12 golden central petals, with a complex of 960 secondary petals arranged around them: thus it is called the "thousand-petaled lotus" in Indian Tantrism. These petals display all the colors of the rainbow, with violet predominating.

In Indian Tantrism this, the *sahasrara* chakra, is described as the "special and highest seat of the Jiva, the soul,"[2] and as such is distinguished from the other chakras which lie along the spinal column. It is most important and reveals both the spiritual quality of the individual and the state of his consciousness. The size, variation in color, speed of rotation, rhythm, degree of brilliance, texture and elasticity, as well as the development of the interconnections with other centers, all indicate the quality and character of the whole personality and the strength of its connection with the inmost self. If the core of the chakra shines very brilliantly, this usually indicates meditation is practiced.

The size of the core, as well as its other characteristics, gives an indication of the individual's ability to expand in consciousness, or even to achieve continuity of consciousness between the waking and sleeping states, for this is the center through which we normally exit in sleep. However, if the core is exceedingly elastic, this may make egress from the body too easy, as in the case of a medium who enters a trance unwittingly.

This is the chakra, in other words, that reveals the stage of conscious evolution in the individual. The religious

2. Arthur Avalon. *The Serpent Power*, Madras: Ganesh & Co., 1958, p. 156.

arts, both East and West, have portrayed this quality symbolically: the Lord Buddha is always depicted with a lofty projection at the top of his head that indicates enlightenment, while the halos of golden light which surround the heads of Christ and the saints symbolize their awakened spirituality. Govinda writes that this center, together with the next two, "go beyond the gross elements (*mahabhuta*) and represent higher dimensions of space, in which the quality of light . . . merges into the psychoenergetic state of *prana* and into the realm of cosmic consciousness."[3] For this reason the crown chakra is looked upon as belonging to a higher order than the other six centers, and is often not included in the list of the chakras, as in Arthur Avalon's work on kundalini yoga, *The Six Centers and the Serpent Power*.

When the etheric interconnections between the crown and the brow centers are open and active, this indicates a degree of clairvoyance, and also that meditation and concentration are practiced. In the physical body, the connection with this center is mainly through the pineal gland, but it influences the whole brain.

At all stages of development, the crown chakra serves as the organ of synthesis.

The Brow Chakra

The brow center, or *ajna* chakra, is composed of ninety-six petals. Located in the center of the forehead midway between the eyes, it is especially interrelated with the crown center. Indeed, in some Tibetan scriptures it is not separately mentioned, but is regarded as part of the "thousand-petalled lotus."

In structure, the brow chakra differs from the other centers in that it appears to be divided into two segments, one half colored rose and yellow, the other blue and purple. (Probably because of this peculiarity, it is described in Indian literature as having two petals.) This center is

---

3. *Op. cit.*, p. 141.

linked with the pituitary gland; interestingly, this gland is also composed of two parts, each of which has a separate function. This is the chakra which is mainly concerned with the integration of ideas and experience with the capacity for organization. (In Indian Tantrism it is said to embody the tattvas of mind and prakriti or primary substance.) It is the organ of visualization and the center of perception, which may be directed upward toward higher things or downward to the mundane world; it thus reflects the twofold nature of the mind.

If the etheric brow chakra is well developed and its interconnections with its astral counterpart are open and active, then clairvoyance of a higher order is possible. When it is interconnected primarily with the throat center, this indicates an active use of the creative imagination.

The Throat Chakra

The throat center (*visuddha* chakra), which is situated just in front of the base of the neck, is silvery blue in color (white in the Indian system) and has sixteen petals. In Buddhist Tantrism, it is associated with the quality of space (*akasa*), the substrate of sound, and the medium of vibration. It is usually about six centimeters in diameter, but becomes much larger in the case of those who use the voice a great deal; it is brighter and faster-moving in singers and those practiced in public speaking. It is also prominent in musicians and composers, and indeed in those engaged in creative work of any kind, for this chakra indicates a sensitivity to color and form as well as sound and rhythm. It could be said that the creative aspect of the self is transmitted from the brow chakra, where it is conceptualized, to the throat chakra, where it is vitalized.

The throat center has links with the crown and brow chakras in certain states of expanded consciousness, and is especially important with respect to the interconnections between the mental and the etheric fields.

The throat chakra's connections with the physical body are through the thyroid and parathyroid glands, to which it supplies energy. From the clairvoyant's point of view, a clear color and a steady rhythm in the etheric throat center indicate a healthy thyroid.

The Heart Chakra

The heart center (*anahata* chakra) is situated at a point midway between the shoulder blades. It is about six centimeters in diameter in the average person, and is composed of twelve petals of a glowing golden yellow. (In Tantrism, its color is described as "smoky.") When the color is clear and the rhythm steady, this indicates a healthy heart condition and a vital physical body. In Tantrism, its characteristic quality is said to be motion.

This chakra is linked with the higher dimensions of consciousness and with one's sense of being, and as noted above it has a close relationship with the twelve golden petals within the crown chakra. The heart center registers the quality and power of love in the individual's life. When a person has transformed personal desires and passions into a wider and more universal compassion and love for his fellows, the heart becomes the focus of energies which were formerly concentrated in the solar plexus. In meditation, the student is encouraged to focus on the heart center, in order to strengthen its connection with the core of the crown chakra. This brings about a state of true balance in the body, for the heart center is really the point of integration in the whole chakra system, and therefore has an important overall balancing effect. The heart center acts as a primary factor in spiritual transformation.

In the physical body, there is a relationship between the heart chakra and the thymus gland, and through it with the immune system. This center is of course related as well with the functioning of the physical heart.

The Solar Plexus Chakra

The solar plexus (*manipura* chakra) is situated in the area of the navel. It has ten petals, and under normal conditions it is multicolored, with light red and green predominating. Fluctuations in rhythm, hyperactivity, and disturbances in the color patterns of this center indicate a person who is overidentified with his emotions, and cannot easily control his feelings.

This chakra is the most important with respect to the connection with the emotional field, since it is at this point that the astral energy enters the etheric field. It is also closely related to the heart and throat chakras.

In the life of an ordinary person, the solar plexus center is probably the most important and active of all the chakras, since it is very much involved in the emotional life. It is active in a person with strong desires, and plays an important role in the projection of personal energy. For this reason, when stress or emotional problems affect the digestive system, this indicates disturbance in the solar plexus area. As might be expected, the physical links with this chakra are principally with the adrenal glands and the pancreas, as well as with the liver and the stomach. This is the center through which most trance-mediums work, and is involved in many less developed types of clairvoyance.

The Spleen Chakra

Descriptions of the chakras vary, and in some traditions the center located above the spleen is listed as one of the seven principal centers; in others, it is considered to be subsidiary. In DVK's observations, the spleen chakra is not perceived as a major chakra, but one which nevertheless plays an important role in the chakra system.

This center has six petals or sections which display a whole spectrum of colors, with yellow and rose-red predominating. Its most important function is to absorb vitality from the general field, modify it, and then distribute it to the other centers. It is believed that each of the colors present in this chakra has a vibratory affinity with the other chakras in which that particular color is dominant (i.e. yellow with the heart, rose-red with the solar plexus, etc.), and that by this means the other chakras are continuously vitalized.

The spleen center is located at the left of the abdomen just below the tenth rib, and is connected with the spleen in the physical body. This center usually has a radiant and glowing appearance. Since it is the main transmitter of prana or life energy to the physical body, its most important function lies in its ability to absorb and distribute vitality.

The Sacral Chakra

In Indian Tantrism, the source from which most of our knowledge of the chakras derives, there are said to be six major centers in the body, plus the "thousand-petalled lotus" or *sahasrara padma*, which we have called the crown chakra. In addition there are many subsidiary centers. According to this system, there is a center (the *svadhisthana* chakra) in the sacral region which governs sexuality. Associated with its six petals, whose color is predominantly red (white in Tibetan Tantrism), are six *vritti* or states of consciousness: credulity, suspicion, disdain, delusion, false knowledge and pitilessness. (c.f. Arthur Avalon, *The Serpent Power*)

According to DVK, this center, like the spleen chakra, has important functions but is not a major center which affects the entire field in the same sense that the other six do. Since the focus of the investigations she and Shafica Karagulla's did together centered primarily upon SK's areas of medical interest, little work was done which involved the sacral chakra.

The Chakra at the Base of the Spine

The root center (*muladhara* chakra) which is situated at the base of the spine, has four petals of a clear orange-red. (In Tantric literature it is said to be connected with the element Earth, also yellow in color.) This center is spoken of as the source or habitat of the kundalini fire, which is coiled up, asleep, in the ordinary human being. The two channels of energy, *ida* and *pingala*, which rise on either side of the major spinal channel, called *sushumna*, originate in this center.

In order to understand the special character of this center, something should be said about the three spinal channels, as they have been identified in the Indian Tantric tradition. It has already been mentioned that the five chakras located in the trunk of the body are interconnected through their roots in the central channel of the spinal column. This central channel, the *sushumna*, originates at the base of the spine and mounts to the medulla oblongata at the base of the brain; it processes the inflow of energy from the etheric field. The other two channels, *ida* and *pingala*, also originate at the base of the spine and end at the base of the brain; they are associated with the outflow of energy.

Ida and *pingala* cross back and forth over the *sushumna* at the points where the five middle chakras are located. This interweaving looks like a living, vibrant caduceus, the ancient symbol of the physician and of the healing arts, which points toward some hidden perception of the pattern of health-giving energies.

The center at the base of the spine, therefore, is particularly associated with the life energy. It is said to respond to that aspect of the self which is frequently called the will, which means the fundamental intentionality of the self. In the developed person, this energy, called kundalini, rises, becomes transmuted and is then linked to the crown chakra.

Subsidiary Chakras

In addition to the major chakras, there are said to be twenty-one minor distributing centers. We will not deal with these in detail, although it may be helpful for the inquirer to know of their existence. These minor centers, which are called *nadis* in Indian Tantrism, differ from true chakras in that they are primarily concentration points where there is a greater flow of energy. They are not associated with any particular glands. The only subsidiary centers which are noteworthy in the context of this study are those in the palm of each hand and in the sole of each foot, as these are important in the practice of healing or therapeutic touch.

The Chakra System

The living process is rich and intricate, a dynamic compounding of many energies and levels of consciousness. The physical body, which represents the final consolidation of all these forces is as complex as the energies that shape and vivify it. Some indications of the play of these energies and their effects upon physical health and disease are the subject of our inquiry.

In physiology, it is recognized that the functions of the body comprise a finely organized and integrated system. If one could observe the energy pattern of the whole etheric body, including its chakras, it too would be seen as a complex but beautifully integrated, mathematically coordinated system. Therefore, if we could extend this concept of organization to include the chakras and their energies as part of the body's functioning, our picture of what constitutes a human being would be much more complete.

VI
The Astral Body and the Emotions

The astral body is the individual field or vehicle of *feeling*, and as such it acts as a bridge between the mind and the physical body. The word "astral" was first used by Paracelsus in the sixteenth century to denote the etheric or vital field, because of its luminous and sparkling appearance. However, in time the use of the word and its meaning changed, and by now it is associated with the level of the emotions, or of thought colored by feelings.

We are aware that there are many kinds of energy at the physical level which interpenetrate the same space without interfering with each other. There are electromagnetic waves such as light waves and radio waves, sound waves, and many others. When the word "higher" is used in connection with wave phenomena, it does not mean "better" or even "more refined"; it simply signifies that the energies under considerastion are characterized by a higher frequency or rate of vibration. It is much like the difference between middle C and high C on a piano. Similarly, the words "above" and "below" are really inadequate to describe a condition wherein etheric, emotional and mental fields interpenetrate each other at every point.

Each of these fields has its own specific qualities. For example, all our emotions, moods and impressions are

47

possible because we are embedded in a universal field called the astral, whose condition is *feeling*. This statement will not be startling to those who have accustomed themselves to the idea that all life is accompanied by a degree of conscious response to the environment, which enables living entities to process information and thus grow and develop. Such conscious response is always accompanied with feeling, whether of pleasure or pain, attraction or fear.

Thus the astral or emotional field is truly universal. It is a fluid world of fast-moving energies, shimmering with color and full of symbols and images that move us with their beauty or fill us with fear and anxiety, since it can be responsive to false and negative ideas as well as to those which are noble and uplifting. But in every case the emotional field is an intrinsic component of human life which needs to be understood and appreciated for what it is.

Within the universal field, every person has an individual emotional field, sometimes called the aura or the astral body.[1] We all write the story of our lives—a record of loves and hates, successes and disappointments, courage, sacrifice and aspiration—in this individual field of the emotions. There are the scars of past sorrows, as well as the bright record of hopes fulfilled. While the individual aura is a picture of all that one feels and has felt, it is a moving picture, not a static one, for it reflects both potentialities realized and possibilities unfulfilled, as well as the dynamics of the here and now. Those who have been near to death testify that their whole life passed in review before their eyes in a blinding flash, signalling that our past is always in some way present in us.

The emotional field is permeated by energy, as are the physical fields, but in this case it is moving much more rapidly, and is therefore perceived as a higher octave of color and sound. The form of the individual emotional field (the astral body, or aura) has certain structural

---

1. DVK will describe different patterns in auras and discuss their meaning in a forthcoming book.

features which correspond to those of the etheric field and the physical body itself. To the clairvoyant, this structure appears as a multicolored aura extending thirty-nine to forty-five centimeters (fifteen to eighteen inches) beyond the physical body. It looks rather like an ovoid, luminous cloud surrounding the body, as though the individual were suspended inside a semitransparent bubble of changing colors and patterns.

These colors indicate not only the quality but also the intensity of the individual's feelings, and whether they are habitual or momentary. Therefore, inner conflicts can be perceived by noting the shade, clarity and position of the colors. Over the years, DVK has learned to distinguish the significance of many shades of colors and the degree of their purity or admixture with other tones.

The texture of the "astral body" is flexible—often described as fluidic—and has the capacity to expand to a considerable extent, but the periphery is clearly marked, even though the material dissipates imperceptibly into the surrounding astral field. The rhythm of the aura is also significant, as it indicates the degree and kind of inter-action with the etheric and mental fields. In health the shape is uniform and well defined, not ragged or wavy at the edges. The section above the diaphragm usually in-dicates the individual's potential—sometimes developed, sometimes not—and the colors in this part of the aura are usually lighter and less intense. The part below the dia-phragm indicates ongoing and active experiences, and here the colors are usually darker, and the texture heavier and more granular. It is impossible to say as yet whether the universal law of gravity may operate in the astral world or not, but it is a fact that the heavier or coarser feelings seem to gravitate to the lower portion of the astral field, while the higher, more expansive feelings are located above the region of the heart.

All these characteristics offer clues to individual idio-syncrasies, and reveal the presence of abnormalities. In our investigations, we regularly used a checklist against which to register our observations. This included seven categories: *quality* (type of energy, density of substance, purity of tone), *texture, form* (whether symmetrical or asymmetrical), *color* (and its location within the aura), *movement* (whether rhythmic or turbulent), *relationship* (to the etheric and mental bodies), and *luminosity*.

The primary characteristic of the aura is dynamism: it is a kaleidoscopic pattern of colors, whose shading and brilliance denote the quality of the emotions. In the average person these vary according to mood, and therefore the colors wax and wane, lighten and darken, and the energies which impel them are in constant motion. For example, an individual who is happy in the presence of a dear friend will display a harmonious pattern of colors suffused with a lovely rose-pink, while during meditation or prayer, the colors may be overlaid with blue and gold. Anger flashes red through the aura like a bolt of lightning, while grief overlays the whole field with a cloud of gray.

There are, however, basic colors which characterize the innate emotional condition or capacity of the individual, and these usually change very slowly. Also, emotions that are sustained over a long period of time remain fairly constant in the aura. If they are negative, such as depression or resentment, they can affect the flow of energy, and this has long-range effects in terms of the condition of the etheric and physical bodies. For example, states of anxiety appear as grayish-blue clouds within the astral field, localized toward the center of the body near the solar plexus chakra. This causes the astral energy to flow inward toward the body, inhibiting the normally free circulation of energy throughout the emotional field. The closer the gray-blue color is to the physical body, the more severe the degree of anxiety and the greater the degree of its impact upon health. When this color tends towards the periphery of the aura, this indicates that the subject is on the way to freeing himself of his anxiety. The activity in the field of the emotional body can be compared to changing conditions in the atmosphere of the earth, when observations from weather satellites verify the areas in which storms are raging. In much the same way, the clairvoyant can perceive the emotional storms which trouble an individual as they disturb his aura.

The colors in the region below the diaphragm indicate the more ordinary and sensate feelings—those which come into play in daily life—while those above this level, especially in the region around the head, indicate intellectual and spiritual qualities.

When the feelings are not under the control or guidance of the self, or responsive to ethical principles, they can be wild and chaotic. In such cases, the person who identifies himself primarily with his emotions can be at the mercy of all its storms and stresses, swinging between extremes of love and hate, joy and sorrow, happiness and pain.

Each human being is constantly creating waves and currents of emotional energy by the ways he responds to the world around him. In our immediate neighborhood, we "people" our space with our emotional images, whether positive, negative or neutral. In turn, these images crowd in upon us and encourage us to repeat the same feelings that fostered them. Thus we develop habitual emotional patterns. The material of the astral world is very impressionable, and responds quickly to the thought-forms or images which we imbue with our feelings. Such images may melt like snow in the sun and vanish, but others may be more enduring and stay with us a long time; these are often seen by clairvoyants surrounding their creator.

If we accept the idea that we are dynamic systems which are constantly receiving and radiating energy, we can understand the degree to which human beings affect one another's emotional fields. This varies, of course, according to the inner stability and integration of the individual. When a person identifies himself with his emotions, he naturally responds readily to the emotions of others. He may be a warm and loving person, but he may also become the victim of other people's emotional disturbances.

Over the years, humanity has produced a great deal of "smog" or debris in the emotional atmosphere. For example, the violence so prevalent in the world today is constantly adding to the pollution of this dimension of life. Those whose emotional attitudes respond to such negative frequencies may be thrown off balance by these disturbing influences, so that their tendencies toward violence become exacerbated. On the positive side, as we look at the emotional climate of the world today, we become aware of the many constructive forces at work. The desire for world peace, the concern for social justice, the compassion for victims of natural or economic disasters, the search for ways to prevent illness and alleviate human suffering—all these feelings resonate to healing forces in the universal emotional field and help create harmony and order.

We might say, therefore, that the astral body of each one of us is the result both of individual emotional activity, whether or not consciously directed, and of interaction with other energies within the general astral field. Every person is in continuous exchange with other people and with the environment as a whole. This open exchange is critically important for health, for even a negative environment need not be damaging if the person involved keeps the interconnection open. The astral field, like all the rest, is universal, and therefore there are no real barriers within it, although local conditions can enhance or inhibit its flow. Thus there are always cleansing and energizing elements in every environment, even in such places as hospitals and prisons, for the individual can reach out beyond his immediate circumstances to the wholeness within nature.

Nevertheless, we draw those elements of the environment towards us to which we are habituated, as like attracts like. Conscious emotional activity establishes patterns of interaction that can, over a period of time, modify an individual's aura. The personal aura or astral body is also affected by the impact of the many types of emotions impinging upon it. Thus our astral environment has subtle but marked effects upon us.

Emotional energy is a powerful force which can be

constructive or destructive, depending upon its use. When controlled and guided by the self, it can become a truly creative force for change and growth. At the present stage in human development, it is not usually perceived in these terms, but current interest in meditation is beginning to show us the power of positive emotions, such as love, to effect self-transformation.

Clairvoyants such as DVK are capable of perceiving the astral aura in great detail, but many other sensitives are able to experience the astral world in a general way. Sometimes such sensitivity is not under control, and this can create difficulties. For example, a person may consciously or unconsciously tune into the feelings of another person so powerfully that he physically feels the other's pain and distress. Many nurses and would-be healers open themselves in this way, by empathizing and taking in the patient's feelings. If the causes of this are unrecognized, such individuals may be considered hypochondriacs, because the physical symptoms can change constantly. On the other hand, such abilities could be of considerable value to a physician in diagnosing the source of an illness. A person can turn a disturbing faculty which may cause emotional exhaustion into a valuable talent, if he realizes that he possesses a type of higher sense perception which can be brought under control.

The Astral Chakras

Within the astral body are to be found seven major astral centers or chakras, which correspond to those on the etheric level. Just as the etheric chakras draw on the energies of the universal etheric field, so these astral centers are open to the great ocean of astral energy in which all living beings are immersed.

As the astral energy flows in and out of these centers from the universal field, it energizes and organizes the astral body or aura. These astral chakras are similar in form to the etheric being petal-like structures clustered around a central core. As with the etheric, the energy flows into this core, circulates through the petals and flows out again into the ocean of astral energy. In the case of the individual human being, the quality of the astral body or individual field pattern depends upon emotional tone and quality. It is as though the person, when interacting with the universal field, absorbs those particular energies with which he is in synchrony, and filters out those which are alien, just as a living organism processes only that information which it is able to utilize. Thus we all leave the imprint of our emotions upon the astral world, and affect the character of the universal field, even though this may be to an infinitesimally small degree in terms of the whole.

The astral chakras also act as interconnections with those at the etheric level, thus integrating the two fields. Depending on the development and degree of integration of the individual, these centers display a harmonious, rhythmic flow of energy, or in contrast, a disturbed, disharmonious pattern which indicates some type of emotional instability. For example, chronic worry produces a disturbance in the solar plexus chakra at the emotional level; this in turn creates a disturbance in the corresponding chakra at the etheric level, which directly affects the digestive tract and liver.

The astral chakras are always brighter than those on the etheric level, but at the same time they are more difficult to describe precisely in respect to such qualities as texture. Little or no variations are observed in elasticity, which appears to be constant. At times the etheric and astral centers may be interrelated and the mental out of harmony; if the color gray appears predominately in an astral center this indicates that there is a blockage between the emotional and mental fields.

In assessing the astral chakras, DVK looks especially at the degree of harmony between the centers in addition to noting whether one center rotates more rapidly or more slowly than the others. If the astral body is generally disturbed, the energy will flow toward one particular chakra, usually that at the solar plexus. It is equally important for health that there be harmony between the astral and etheric centers. When there is a steady and harmonious rhythm between the astral and etheric chakras, a good inner relationship is indicated, whereas disharmony and dissonance may lead to disease.

A break in the petals or in the core of one of the astral centers, leading to a leakage of energy, will tend to make that center and the energy supplied to the corresponding part of the body more vulnerable; this may or may not lead to illness or some kind of serious physical condition.

The Crown Chakra

Unlike the etheric, the astral body has no visible counter-parts of the physical organs, such as the spleen or the intestinal tract. There is, however, an exchange of energy. For example, if the flow of astral energy is dull in the crown center, one should expect serious mental disorders or even extreme mental deficiency. If, on the other hand, the etheric and astral levels match in color and brilliance, this indicates that the thinking processes are clear and lively. The reflection of the pineal gland may appear as a golden color in the astral body, but there is no true counter-part of the organ.

The Throat Chakra

This center is particularly associated with rhythm and sound. In those who are clairaudient, or sensitive to sounds which are physically inaudible, the petals of this center will be larger than average and more luminous. When diagnosing, the main factor to be looked for in connection with this center is its degree of harmony with the etheric chakra.

The Heart Chakra

In individuals who meditate regularly, the heart center is larger than usual, for it expands easily. It also tends to be more luminous, and its rhythmic movement is speeded

up. The connections with the higher levels of consciousness described in Chapter VII are also more apparent.

The Solar Plexus Chakra

This is the most active center of emotional energy in
the majority of people. It is the bridge between the emotions and the physical/etheric, its closest physical connection being with the stomach and the whole gastrointestinal tract. DVK has theorized that the astral solar
plexus chakra acts as a shock absorber between the intake
of astral energy and its dispersal through the body.

The colors of this chakra are somewhat variable: in an
integrated person, the green indicates balance; a somewhat different shade pertains to sympathy or adaptability;
a mixture of yellow and green shows interest in expressing
ideas in physical form. Often inventors and designers
have this color combination. Also there is an entirely
different shade of sickly yellowish-green which indicates
jealousy, while yellow mixed with gray implies frustration
in connection with work.

The Chakra at the Base of the Spine

This center is closely related to the crown chakra, and
is therefore associated with the spiritual development of
the individual. If there is integration between these two
centers, the energy rises from the root chakra without
impediment or disturbance, particularly in the emotional
and etheric fields.

The Astral Spine and Brain

The astral energy normally enters the individual field
via the solar plexus chakra, and may move in either of two
directions, depending upon whether or not there is obstruction to its flow along the astral "spine," in which the
chakras have their roots. In a normal, healthy state, the
astral energy flows upward towards the head, but when

obstructed it will turn and flow downward, increasing sexual activity. At the same time there will be a diminution of the astral energy in the brain, leading to a disturbance in the balance of control.

The astral spinal energy, like its etheric counterpart, rises from the chakra at the base of the spine and flows upward to the medulla oblongata in three streams which correspond with the *ida, pingala* and *sushumna*. DVK has described these as follows: The stream on the right side of the astral spine rises from the right side of the core of the chakra at the base of the spine and flows upward to the back of the head in a stream approximately one centimeter in width. Its color is pale blue (whereas the etheric counterpart is blue-green). The stream on the left side of the spine duplicates that on the right, but its color is pink (whereas the etheric is a darker yellow-red). The energy which flows through the central portion of the astral spine arises from the very heart of the base spinal chakra, moves upward and bifurcates at the area near the medulla oblongata, at which point the two divisions cross each other, the energy on the right going to the left brain, and that on the left to the right brain. This central spinal stream is brighter than the other two streams, opalescent and many-colored, with a great deal of yellow and orange. If it is very bright with a predominance of yellow, this indicates a state of health.

With respect to the brain, at the astral level the energy is structured differently from the etheric, and there appears to be some connection between the cerebellum, the pineal gland and the crown chakra. There is normally a tremendous amount of energy in the brain at the astral level.

Readers will doubtless notice that we have not described the function of all the astral chakras. This is because our research was confined to areas of the body associated with particular chakras mentioned above. There are others which we have not described.

VII
Higher Dimensions of Consciousness

The third aspect or facet of the personal self is the instrument through which the mind finds expression; in theosophical and esoteric literature this is traditionally called the mental body. As previously mentioned, just as the emotional or astral level has a higher frequency and subtler state of materiality than the etheric, so the mental is finer-grained and faster-moving than the astral. However, it should be remembered that the mental field interpenetrates both the astral and the etheric at every point, and the mental body also conforms to these vehicles in structure. The mental dimension is in constant interplay with other aspects of the personality throughout life, and its energy permeates every experience, even when we are not engaged in intellectual pursuits or even consciously thinking.

The energy which pours into the mental chakras from the inexhaustible reservoir of the universal mental field circulates through the mental chakra system in much the same manner as at the astral and etheric levels. But the mind is more complex than the emotions; it has in fact two primary aspects or functions which make possible the subtlety, originality and conceptual power of the mind, at the same time that it can lead us into false reasoning and self-delusion. Because of its multifaceted nature, the habits and patterning of the mind can affect the disease process adversely, but it can also be a powerful force for health, growth and change.

At the level of everyday experience, the mind is the instrument which integrates and interprets the stream of sensory data which flood into us from every side. All these data are processed and evaluated by the brain/mind and applied to our behavior. This aspect of the mind delivers the common sense we all use in the business of daily living, and which perceives the relationships between things, people and events that give these phenomena their context and meaning.

The conceptual or abstract mind cognizes meaning of a higher order: the ideas which give events their significance; the unities which underlie life's variables; the structure, proportion, balance, harmony, order and lawfulness of nature; the relationship between human life and the earth, as well as between the individual and mankind. This dimension of the mind is a universal human attribute, even though it may not be developed to the same degree in all of us.

The human mental body is an ovoid like the astral, but it is considerably larger and less dense. Its colors and quality are good indicators of the individual's interests and mental powers, whether latent or active, for sometimes the capacities we are born with do not mature during life. All this shows up in the mental body, just as the astral aura accurately reveals the emotional life.

Because the mental and emotional fields are so closely interconnected, the mind is colored by emotion, just as the feelings are conditioned by thought. This is a universal characteristic, but when it is unbalanced or out of control the condition may become pathological. However, if the mind is not hampered by emotional stresses, it is a fine and flexible instrument for integrating and assimilating all levels of personal experience: mental, emotional and physical.

The physical brain, much like a supercomputer, registers, stores and retrieves what the mind discovers or originates.

The view of the mind/brain relationship which emerges from our research is very different from that generated by most psychophysiological theorizing. Far from being a product of brain activity, the distillation of meaning and the interpretation of experience are seen to derive from a deeper level of the self. Such insight is then developed rationally by the mind and related to other knowledge, while the brain, which is the mind's instrument or physical partner, registers the information. In other words, the mind is dependent upon the brain for physical expression, but it also transcends the brain mechanism and can to some extent compensate for its defects.

The mental body extends about ninety centimeters (three feet) beyond the periphery of the physical body, and interpenetrates both the etheric and the astral bodies. The individual who perceives the "I" more in terms of his thoughts than his feelings usually has a mental body that is brighter and more vital than the average, and of finer texture. When such a person is using the mind, energy moves more swiftly in and out of the mental chakras, and the whole mental body becomes more lively and luminous.

The speed with which the energy moves in and out of the chakras, the luminosity of the colors, the rhythm and the degree of brightness of the different chakras all indicate the quality of the mental body and the areas of special development.

When there is a harmonious relationship from the mental level through the emotional to the etheric, the flow of energy through the chakras displays a rhythmic and unimpeded pattern. Unfortunately, many human beings are subject to periodic mental or emotional storms and stresses, and these have their effects in the etheric and physical bodies.

The energies at the mental level are discharged at a more rapid rate and with more volatility than the lower energies. In fact, when energy flows actively in and out this lights up the field around the individual and this affects his environment in direct proportion to the strength of the thought. Thus ideas which are charged with mental power strongly influence other individuals. This may or may not be directly related to the truth of the ideas themselves: grand ideas stand the test of history and contribute to the growth of human culture, but mistaken ideas can dominate large groups of people when these are projected with great force and conviction, as was the case in Nazi Germany.

The transformative power of thought when it is reinforced by conviction is well known. Religious conversion is one example, but on a lesser level, the ability to break long-standing habits, such as smoking, results from the power of the mind to change behavior. We no longer believe the dictum, "I think, therefore I am," but we realize that what we think strongly affects us, whether as individuals, members of organizations or citizens of a nation. In fact, national purpose or character is largely dependent upon the way a people thinks of itself.

How are such widespread ideas transmitted? The effect is partly achieved through written argument and speech, but even more through sharing a common vision or worldview based upon a strong mental image. Such a mental image has come to be known as a thought-form. The spread of ideas is achieved through the mind's ability to construct a powerful and well-defined image within the mental body, and then direct it toward its object with clarity and intensity. This ability to project one's thoughts clearly is an important factor in successful teaching, as well as in political life. But the ability to create strong thought-forms can also react upon us negatively, for if they become too rigid they can surround and imprison us within a wall of our own making, thus preventing the inrush of new ideas and fresh mental energy. We then become ideologues, or fanatics who reject all but their own interpretations of truth.

Some clairvoyants are able to see the thought-forms within an individual's mental body. A discussion with the late Phoebe Payne Bendit, who was acknowledged to be a competent and trained clairvoyant, helped to clarify this matter. She recounted the case of a man who came to her claiming that he was possessed by several great musicians who had passed on, and that other clairvoyants had corroborated his claim. But when Phoebe Bendit observed him carefully, she found that these figures were not those long-gone musicians at all, but rather the man's wish-fulfillment thoughts that he had charged with his own hopes and desires. She warned his family that he was headed toward a dangerous mental illness, and unfortunately this materialized a few months later, when he was diagnosed as a paranoid schizophrenic and admitted to a mental hospital.

When Mrs. Bendit was asked how she differentiated the patient's thought-form from an actual astral entity, she replied: "How would you differentiate between a living person and a statue? Isn't one obviously alive, while the other is not? The same holds true on the astral and mental planes. An actual person, even though dead, has a quality of vitality about him, so that he moves, changes and responds to what is going on. In contrast, a thought-form is lifeless and static, and its energy comes from the astral and mental fields of the individual who harbors it."

The great advantage of being able to see thought-forms is that we can become aware of what we are generating, and thus change them to more constructive images. But even if we cannot see them clairvoyantly, when we realize that our thoughts have the ability to affect others directly and that we energize them with our emotions, we begin to feel a degree of responsibility for our thoughts that was previously reserved only for our actions, and indeed come to acknowledge that thoughts *are* action of a kind, in that they affect behavior.

The Effect of Visualization

The ability to use our minds constructively in order to achieve good health and personal self-transformation is the subject of literally hundreds of books currently being offered to the public. Most of these suggest methods that can be used with some degree of success, for the mere conviction that one can effect personal change and growth is enough to start the process moving. Because of the interest in various techniques which employ visualization and different forms of relaxation and/or meditation, we conducted an exploratory inquiry into the ways students use some of these techniques.

We discovered that a few members of the group we studied had no ability to perceive a mental image. When they closed their eyes, they were aware of nothing but blankness and darkness. Most of the students, however, were able to hold in their mind's eyes the object they were asked to visualize, such as the face of a friend or a simple colored geometric figure. When they were asked how they perceived this mental image, most of them said they visualized the object outside themselves, at a distance of about twenty centimeters in front of their eyes, as though they were reading a book. Others reported that they visualized the object inside their heads, usually in the frontal lobes of the brain, although a few said they saw it in the back of the brain in the occipital region. There was also a very small group that said they could not only think of the object but could also perceive it as a picture flashing before their eyes without specific localization.

In most cases the mental image which was formed remained static. Although holding on to such an image may be an excellent exercise in mental concentration, it will have little effect on the mental, astral and etheric fields unless it is energized and becomes dynamic. For example, if a person is emotionally upset and is told to visualize a green disk over the solar plexus area in order to help him calm down, it should be perceived as a green light flowing into his solar plexus and thence harmonizing the whole abdominal region. In other words, if the thought-form is to be effective, it must maintain its dynamics.

In another experiment, DVK was asked to observe the effect on VPN's throat chakra as she visualized certain geometrical forms and colors. DVK was not told what symbols were being used, but was merely to observe their effects on this chakra, which was somewhat leaky.

At first, VPN visualized a deep blue-violet diamond-shaped pattern a few centimeters in size and localized in front of the throat chakra. DVK reported no effect. The second symbol visualized was a golden diamond-shaped object. DVK reported that the image was speeding up the throat chakra very slightly, but that the effect was more apparent on the astral level than on the etheric, where the symbol did not seem to hit the core of the center. When a silver-blue diamond was visualized, it too affected the astral chakra but not the etheric. The conclusion seemed to be that when visualization is a purely mental exercise, it does not seem to affect the chakras. On the other hand, they do respond to the visualization of a symbol which has some significance or inner meaning for the practitioner, as attested by the effective use of visualization in patients.

The Mental Chakras

The chakras within the mental body correspond to those on the astral and etheric levels, processing energy and acting as media of exchange with the universal mental field. Each mental chakra is also closely linked with its higher frequency counterpart on the intuitional (buddhic) level. All together, they form a closely integrated system which could be imaged as a four-dimensional grid, in which the energies move laterally through each chakra system and also vertically between the different levels. The energy on the mental level moves more swiftly and at a higher frequency than on the emotional, just as the emotional is higher than the etheric.

The energy of the mental field is stepped down as it passes through the chakras, and can in this way have a direct effect on the physical body if it is not blocked at the emotional level, which is sometimes the case.

The frequency of the energy which flows into the

chakras depends on the mental development of the individual. If there is a disturbance in one of the mental centers, it will be transmitted to the emotional and etheric levels, but it is more usual for the disturbance to occur at the astral level. An astral disturbance will not only affect the etheric chakra but also inhibit the energy coming in from the mental level. The whole process is very complex.

When there is a harmonious relationship among the various aspects of the personality, the energy flows from level to level rhythmically and freely. Unfortunately, such a balance is rather rare, since people interrupt the harmony in a variety of ways: through stress, anxiety, mental rigidity and emotional storms, to name only a few. If such conditions persist the physical body is eventually affected adversely.

As in the astral chakras, the speed with which the energy moves in and out of the vortices, the luminosity of the colors, the rhythm and the brightness of the different centers all indicate the quality and power of the mind, and the areas of special development or ability.

The Causal Body

Although the causal body was not the subject of our investigations, DVK found it impossible not to refer to it occasionally, since the fundamental reality within every human being is what we call the Self, although it is also known as the Soul or Spirit. The highest vesture of the Self, which is known as buddhi (insight, wisdom, "clear seeing" or *prajna*), is termed "causal" because, according to esotericism, it carries the Self's fundamental intentionality to *be*, and this is the ultimate cause of our existence.

By whatever name, this is the real, enduring dimension of true being in each of us—that which persists through all the changes and vicissitudes of our life, and gives it meaning and continuity.

This spiritual dimension is the source of all that is best in us, and can exert a powerful influence for growth and self-transformation. According to the doctrine of reincarnation, those fruits of experience which we have transformed into enduring qualities mark the growth or evolution of the individual self. These are retained from life to life within the causal body which becomes a composite of the highest qualities of the Self: insight, intuition or direct knowing, creativity, intentionality, aspiration to God or the Good, and the purest forms of love and compassion. It can be called the true vehicle of self-awareness, if by that we mean universal consciousness focused in the individual self.

Seen clairvoyantly, the causal body is pale and ethereal, with iridescent colors like those in a soap bubble. It was called the Augoeides by the Greeks, the luminous radiation of the Spiritual Self, of which incarnate life is but the shadow. But it is also termed "causal" because it gathers together the fruits of our long struggles and sacrifices to grow in understanding, and in these lie the true causes of what we are here and now—the seeds of our qualities of mind and heart. At this level, the Self is not constrained by the usual limits of time and space and causality, but is able to experience the universality of life and to perceive meanings and interrelationships which are often hidden from us during physical existence.

The causal body does not disintegrate after death as the astral and mental bodies eventually do, but persists from life to life. In Tibet, tulkus or "incarnations" are said to be saints or teachers who are reborn again and again with access to the same memories and capacities they had before. Although such cases are rare, there is within the causal dimension the distillation of all earthly experience, and because it is ever-present, this record is accessible to one who has the ability to perceive it.

In the case of some of our patients, it was obvious to DVK that the problems she encountered were rooted at levels beyond the physical, the emotional or even the mental, and she therefore searched for their explanation more deeply, within the causal dimension.

3

Clairvoyance as a Diagnostic Tool

VIII
The Background of Clairvoyant Investigation

Materials obtained from clairvoyant research in this century are meager, and what there are, have for the most part been developed through personal initiative and without much attention to the need for verification. Consequently, although some literature on clairvoyant investigation is available, it is not of the kind to claim the attention of the scientific community. Nonetheless, it is important to note that, although the faculty of clairvoyance is rare, it is by no means an isolated phenomenon. For this reason, some survey of the historical material available to us may serve as context for the research offered here.

We shall confine ourselves to Westerners who have testified to paranormal abilities in their lives and in their work, leaving out accounts of Eastern seers. These are of course far more numerous, but since they are embedded in a culture which has always accepted the presence of unseen forces and higher dimensions of perception, little systematic effort has been made to correlate such accounts with empirical evidence.

In the East, paranormal abilities are taken for granted as a concomitant or byproduct of training in yogic practices, and therefore the stress is always upon self-development, rather than the acquisition of powers per se. Yogis may be able to suspend their vital functions for days or weeks, live practically without food, maintain their bodily heat while sitting on a snow drift, levitate or leave their physical bodies at will, all without attracting much attention or arousing anyone's interest in documenting such practices.

In the West, however, paranormal abilities have traditionally been suspect, tainted with witchcraft and demonism at worst, or with hallucination or self-deception at best. The Saints and seers alone were exempt, since their visionary experiences were sanctified by a religious setting. With the rise of the Enlightenment in the eighteenth century and materialistic science in the nineteenth, the Western world-view had little room for anything that could not be explained in terms of physical reality.

The end of the nineteenth century, however, saw the close of the era of the old physicalism. The discovery of X-rays and radioactivity came soon after a wave of interest in psychic phenomena, mediumship and after-death communications swept across England and America. Trance-mediumship, materializations, apports, psychic photography, the survival of the astral form after death and similar phenomena were all subjected to intensive investigation by persons of repute and critical judgment. Such well-known names as Sir William Crookes and Arthur Conan Doyle, along with the British Society for Psychical Research, are associated with the extensive investigations that were undertaken in many different aspects of psychism. Some of the pathfinders in this unexplored field are of great interest to those of us who are attempting to put present research into context, so that it does not appear to be an irrepeatable phenomenon.

We shall begin this brief and acknowledgeably incomplete list with a physician, Philippus Theophrastus Bombast of Hohenheim, better known as Paracelsus, who lived and practiced at the beginning of the sixteenth century. He is believed to have traveled to India, where he studied esoteric principles. Certainly he was the first post-Renaissance writer to describe the sevenfold constitution of man, earthbound spirits and the nature of the higher bodies. It was he who coined the term "astral," meaning starry, although he applied it to what we now speak of as the etheric or vital field. From his writings it is apparent that he could see the etheric field and that he used his perceptions in medicine and healing. These practices brought him both fame and obloquy, and he is believed to have died from poisoning as a result of his unorthodox ideas.

Emanuel Swedenborg, best remembered for the church named after him, was a gifted and versatile scientist, noted as a palaeontologist, physicist and physiologist who studied the functions of the brain and of the ductless glands. In middle life, he left physical research for psychical investigation, for he testified that he had long been instructed by dreams, experienced visions and heard mysterious conversations—showing that his gifts included both clairvoyance and clairaudience. After an extraordinary spiritual experience, he devoted his life to theology and the study of the Christian scriptures, which he interpreted in the light of his insights.

The most remarkable psychic of recent times is undoubtedly Helena Petrovna Blavatsky, founder of the modern theosophical movement. From birth she was the focus of extraordinary events and mysterious phenomena. Although not a medium of the ordinary kind (for she in fact attacked mediumship as it was practiced in her day), she was able to act as a conscious channel and instrument for conveying the teachings of her Masters, whom she served as amenuensis in the writing of many notable works, including *The Secret Doctrine*, which became the source book for all subsequent theosophical and esoteric teachings. Her remarkable powers have been attested by large numbers of people, who saw her materialize objects, communicate with the unseen, control elemental spirits, and describe other dimensions of existence while she was in full waking consciousness.

In her voluminous writings, she frequently stressed the fact that there is nothing "supernatural" in the universe, and that paranormal abilities are responses to natural laws and forces which have not yet been discovered by science. She predicted in the 1880s that the prevailing materialism would be shattered before the end of the century, and that there would be a new understanding of the nature of matter itself. Many of her statements which were completely unacceptable to the science of her day have now become part of the contemporary world-picture. Her prophetic proposals include the concepts that every cell of the body contains that form's blueprint, and that life is incipient in all matter, appearing spontaneously when the conditions are appropriate.

Blavatsky's greatest contribution to the emergence of a new world-view was a comprehensive metaphysics which is able to overcome the dichotomy between consciousness and energy that has for so long plagued the West, by showing that they are complementary aspects of an underlying reality. This hypothesis furnishes the framework within which the subtler and more problematic aspects of nature and man can be integrated, making our hopes for an holistic world-view more realizable.

This metaphysics, conjoined with the new physics, has furnished the ground for describing the higher dimensions of human consciousness as universal fields, a development which we owe to F.L. Kunz, founder of the Center for Integrative Education and its innovative journal, *Main Currents in Modern Thought*. As a result, although this area of research has as yet scarcely been broached, it now becomes possible to systematize and explain phenomena which were formerly difficult to reconcile with scientific or medical findings. Whether or not Blavatsky's contributions become widely acknowledged, all subsequent developments in the field of the paranormal may be said to have originated in her revolutionary work.

Another remarkable woman, who was drawn into the theosophical movement by her interest in Blavatsky's writings, was Dr. Annie Besant. A social reformer who worked vigorously for human causes with Charles Bradlaugh in the Fabian Society, she became President of The Theosophical Society and moved to India, where she established a number of educational institutions, founded the well-known journal *New India*, and was imprisoned by the British for her efforts in behalf of India's independence. She developed clairvoyance when she was in her late forties, and collaborated with C.W. Leadbeater in the writing of several books based on their observations, notably *Occult Chemistry, Thought Forms,* and *Man and His Bodies*. Later, when she became immersed in her public work in India, she deliberately shut off her psychic faculties, and ceased to pursue her clairvoyant investigations.

Charles W. Leadbeater has been mentioned already as a remarkably gifted clairvoyant who wrote extensively about his observations, especially concerning after-death conditions. His descriptions of the subtler dimensions of man—as in *The Chakras* (from which our illustrations are taken), which remains one of the most widely read books in the subject, and in *Man Visible and Invisible*, which describes the features of the human aura—are classics in the field of paranormal studies. His book *Thought Forms*, which holds that the mind has the ability to create tangible forms perceptible to sensitives, exerted considerable influence over many artists, such as Mondrian and Kandinsky.

Other well-known clairvoyants include Geoffrey Hodson, who is best known for his books about the angelic kingdom, such as *The Kingdom of the Gods*. He also did a considerable amount of medical research, some results of which are incorporated in his book *An Occult View of Health and Disease*. Perhaps because he was not born clairvoyant, but developed the faculty during his adult life, he gave the process considerable attention, as in his *Science of Seership*.

Phoebe Payne Bendit's clairvoyance was principally of the etheric level, and in conjunction with her husband, Laurance Bendit, who was a physician, she wrote several studies of health and disease based on her observations. She also published a book called *Man's Latent Powers*, in which she described the differences she observed between conscious clairvoyance and trance-mediumship.

There are a number of other figures whose contributions are primarily philosophical and theoretical, but in which occult investigations have played an important part. Among the most prominent of these is Rudolf Steiner, founder of the Anthroposophical Society. This movement holds many concepts in common with theosophy, but with special innovations and emphases, such as the application of metaphysics to mathematics, education and the arts. Steiner, a remarkably versatile man, was a scientist who used his clairvoyance to study nature, and as a result he developed theories about plant compatibility which have resulted in companion planting to prevent disease. His recommendations are still practiced in farming projects sponsored by the Anthroposophical Society, while his educational principles are basic to the successful Steiner and Waldorf schools, as well as to the Society's fine work with the retarded.

Alice Bailey was another teacher, still influential in the field of esotericism, who was also recognized for her telepathic abilities. She is best known for a large body of writings which she stated were received telepathically from a Tibetan Adept known as Djual Khul. These writings stem from the work of H.P. Blavatsky, but differ from them in many details; they must, as the author herself has stated, be judged by their quality rather than by their source of inspiration.

A somewhat different kind of paranormal ability was that which Nikola Tesla exhibited. Preeminent in the development of electrical instruments, he recorded that he had a vision of how electricity might be generated from waterfalls, and this was fulfilled twenty years later, in 1896, with a dynamo at Niagara Falls. It is said he was able to produce earthquakes at will, as well as lightning flashes forty meters long; he once lighted two hundred electric lamps twenty-five miles away, without any conductors. *The American Encyclopedia* describes him thus: "He had a way of intuitively sensing hidden scientific secrets, and employing his inventive talent to prove his hypotheses."

Turning to scientists who explored the field of the paranormal in various ways, we must note the work of Baron Karl von Reichenbach, a chemist, who was the discoverer of paraffin, creosote and pitacol, as well as an authority on meteorites and an industrialist whose empire stretched from the Danube to the Rhine. In 1845 he published seven controversial papers entitled "Researches on Magnetism, Electricity, Heat and Light and Their Relation to Vital Power," in which he testified to evidence for what he called the "odic light." He made careful and detailed observations of subjects who were able to perceive this light, which was similar to the vital field, but his work was rejected by the European scientific community, although accepted and translated into English by William Gregory, M.D.

Sir William Crookes (1832-1919), English chemist and physicist, discovered thallium, constructed the radiometer, and through his researches developed his theory of "radiant matter," or matter in a "fourth state." His inquiries into the nature of the rare earths, especially yttrium, led him to the theory that all elements have been produced by evolution from one primordial stuff. He was a keen student of psychic phenomena, as he testified in his work *Researches in the Phenomena of Spiritualism*, and sought to effect some correlation between the paranormal and ordinary physical laws.

Others who should be mentioned as contributing to a scientific approach to the study of psychic phenomena are Walter J. Kilner, Alexis Carrel, M.D., Professor T. Fukurai of the Imperial University of Tokyo (who lost his position because of his interest in the field), Joseph Banks Rhine, whose research into telepathy and clairvoyance was founded on statistical evaluation, Oscar Bagnall, a biologist at Cambridge University who studied the human aura, and Sir George Hubert Wilkins, an explorer who carried out experimental work in telepathy. Special mention should be made of Edgar Cayce, whose outstanding medical work is still the subject of research and investigation.

A number of researchers have made serious efforts to

validate psychic phenomena through various kinds of
testing. Evelyn M. Penrose was a sensitive who worked
for the Canadian and Australian governments to find
sources of water, as well as minerals and archeological
sites. Andrija Puharich, M.D., and Dr. Charles Osis of the
Society for Psychical Research have extensively documented the paranormal abilities of a number of psychics.
The United States government as well as the Soviets have
quietly pursued the possibilities of research into the as
yet unexplored powers of the mind to deflect laser beams,
modify magnetic fields, see at a distance and move objects.
Sheila Ostrander and Lynn Schroeder documented the
Russian efforts in this field in their book *Psychic Discoveries
Behind the Iron Curtain* (1970), while Russell Targ and
Harold Puthoff reported on American research in *Mind
Reach* (1977), and more recently Targ collaborated with
Keith Harary in *The Mind Race* (1984).

In recent years, a number of people endowed with
various forms of higher sense perception have collaborated
with researchers in several fields. Stephan A. Schwartz
describes in his book, *The Alexandria Project*, how psychics
with the ability of "remote viewing," or seeing at a distance,
contributed to the success of his archaeological project,
their impressions being later confirmed by work on the
site. Others have used the same abilities in finding under-
water treasures in sunken ships. In another field, John
Taylor, a physicist and mathematician at Kings College,
London, described in *Superminds* (1975) how metals
broken psychically differ in structure from those broken
physically.

In the field of health and healing, Dr. Bernard Grad
of McGill University in Montreal, Canada, studied the
beneficial effects of healing energies on both plants and
mice in the laboratory. He described the effects achieved
by a noted healer, Colonel Oskar Estabany, in speeding
the rate of healing in wounds of mice, as well as in sprouting
damaged plant seeds. These tests were all conducted
under controlled conditions. Dr. Grad also found that
flowers wilted more rapidly when in contact with

mentally depressed patients than in the presence of normal persons.

Continuing this research, Sister Justa Smith developed a project whose aim was to compare the activity of the enzyme trypsin when treated by Colonel Estabany's laying-on-of-hands with exposure to the effects of a magnetic field. The colonel was asked to put his hands around a stoppered glass flask containing the enzyme solution for a maximum of seventy-five minutes. The results were published by Sister Justa in a paper entitled "Paranormal Effects on Enzyme Activity," which concluded that "the evidence presented indicates that exposure of a trypsin solution to the healing power of the laying-on-of-hands as performed by Colonel Estabany is qualitatively and quantitatively similar to that of a magnetic field. This would imply that healing can be induced by a magnetic field." The research thus indicates that biological changes may occur when in contact with the hands of some healers, although not all healers were able to duplicate Colonel Estabany's accomplishment (Chapter XVI.)

To conclude this brief survey, we should mention the importance of changing attitudes which are gradually becoming evident in the scientific community, and which are much more hospitable to supersensory research. The most revolutionary development is the acknowledgment that consciousness plays a critical and pervasive role in physical existence. Since many scientists are not yet ready to take this role into consideration, we would like to offer a few statements which support it.

Prof. George Wald, Nobel Laureate in Physics, said in a 1985 talk: "It will never be possible to identify physically the presence or absence of consciousness.... [It is] a time-less and pervasive property, a complementary aspect of all reality." Addressing the famous question raised by Descartes with respect to the fundamental dualism of mind and matter, Eric Jantsch writes in *The Self-Organizing Universe*: "Mind is immanent ... in the processes in which the [living] system organizes and renews itself and evolves" (p. 162). And in the same vein, quantum physicist Erwin

Schroedinger wrote in *What Is Life?*: "Consciousness is associated with the *learning* of the living substance" (p. 103). In their book *Einstein's Space and Van Gogh's Sky*, Larry LeShan and Henry Margenau quote A.S. Eddington, a physicist who wrote in 1926 that "the division of the external world into a material world and a spiritual world is superficial" (p. 236). Discussing characteristics of the domain of consciousness, they conclude that "the observables will be different in sharpness and distinguishability from those in the sensory realm. There are no 'things' in this realm, only 'processes.' " Also, "observables have 'limited access'—that is, they can only be observed by one person—in contrast to the 'public access' of observables in many other realms." These statements certainly have bearing upon the materials of our study.

Finally, we include the following quotation from physicist David Bohm's book *Wholeness and the Implicate Order*, which suggests the best contemporary rationale for our research:

> The easily accessible explicit content of consciousness is included within a much greater implicit (or implicate) background. This in turn evidently has to be contained in a yet greater background which may include not only neuro-physiological processes at levels of which we are not generally conscious but also a yet greater background of unknown (and indeed ultimately unknowable) depths of inwardness that may be analogous to the "sea" of energy that fills the sensibly perceived "empty" space. (p. 210)

Our investigations certainly support this view. The fact that neurophysiological processes are accompanied (or often preceded) by changes in the content of consciousness is an important conclusion derived from the study; even more striking, perhaps, is the "sea of energy" which not only pervades "empty" space but is focused and processed by those organs of consciousness called the chakras.

The idea that consciousness and matter are inseparable concomitants of existence is an esoteric or theosophical concept which helps to furnish both a context and an explanatory principle for paranormal phenomena. The research offered here has a dual role: it tests the validity of extrasensory perception; but even more importantly, it reveals some of the dimensions of consciousness and the interplay between these dimensions and those of physical reality.

IX

The Use of Clairvoyance in Research

In Chapter II we suggested that higher sense perception can offer a more complete picture of human functioning than is so far available, and also that such perceptions can become incorporated into the body of accepted knowledge only if they meet the test of empirical evidence. In our work there was a consistent effort to test the research against available medical records, but it is obvious that the control was far from perfect. Nevertheless, since such exploratory procedures are necessary in order to open up a new field, we want to share with the reader some details of the way we worked together and the problems we encountered.

During the first two years of our research, presumably healthy people were observed, in order to get a general idea what it is that DVK perceives. With increased observations, many factors which intervene when disease is present became apparent. This helped to increase our knowledge of the characteristics of the chakras and of the fields which they epitomize.

Prior to our collaboration, DVK had seen patients mainly at the request of their medical doctors when she was asked for her evaluation. The emphasis was primarily on observations of the astral vehicles of the patients, in order to discover the causes of the emotional problems which were a factor in their diseases. In our work together, however, she was asked to focus her clairvoyant vision primarily at the etheric level, in order to observe the structure and function of the endocrine glands and the chakras which control them. The accuracy of her etheric sight was to be determined by the correlation of her observations with the patients' case histories.

DVK did not make a diagnosis as such, since she had no knowledge of medicine, nor was she familiar with the appropriate terms to describe what she saw. But her observations of the etheric abnormalities in the chakras and their corresponding endocrine glands left no doubt as to their accuracy. Over a period of time, she was presented with many rare medical cases, such as those in which the pituitary gland had been surgically excised for therapeutic purposes in patients suffering from cancer of the breast or thyroid (a practice in favor at the time). Most of the medically documented cases were obtained from the outpatient endocrine clinic of a prestigious medical school in New York City; other data were obtained in California.

DVK was asked to observe the chakras and the endocrine glands related to them, regardless of whether they appeared normal or abnormal. A chart was developed to record her findings, and this procedure was followed consistently.

DVK never spoke to any of the patients. Her position at the back of the outpatient clinic, about twenty feet from the subjects, often precluded her from even seeing their faces. In any one morning session, two or three patients were randomly selected for her evaluation. She was asked to observe two or three of the etheric centers and the corresponding endocrine glands, and also to assess the patients' general etheric fields. It usually took two to three hours to evaluate a single patient, if all the chakras were studied.

The procedure was as follows: DVK filled out the chart form[1] with her observations of the patients, while SK's

---

1. This form appears in the case histories which are included in the appendix.

task was to obtain the medical charts of the patients under study and extract the relevant data. A few hours later we would compare notes and correlate the information.

Working at the outpatient clinic was not an easy task for DVK, because of her sensitivity to those who were filled with anxiety and suffering pain, but we had no choice if we were to obtain the documentation we needed. The work was much easier, however, in the cases we saw privately outside the hospital atmosphere. It should be mentioned that during the course of this research, we never charged a fee to anyone, whether seen in the clinic or privately. The research was supported by grants from foundations or friends, for when working in new and unorthodox fields, it is essential to remain free from outside control as well as pristine in one's rejection of financial gain.

The Mechanics of Clairvoyant Perception

Quite a number of people can see the general outlines of the etheric body, which extends about five centimeters beyond the physical, but very few have the ability to perceive the details of the etheric energy field and its centers.

Some sensitives use various techniques to focus their awareness. For example, Frances Farrelly, who has a range of psychic abilities, uses a mechanism which she calls the "stick." (See Chapter XVI for a more extended account of this sensitive's accomplishments.) When she rubs her fingers on a piece of wood or plastic, while at the same time concentrating on a question for which she seeks an answer, she gets a feeling of stickiness if the answer is affirmative, but no change if it is negative. She has used the same method when dowsing on a map in order to locate water or minerals. Since the answer is merely yes or no, she must be very precise in her mental questions.

This "stickiness" feeling has been elevated to the rank of a "scientific language" known as Digital Excitation Response (DER) at the Stanford Research Institute, a U.S.

Government research center. It has been demonstrated that none of the so-called radionic instruments which use the "stick" as part of their mechanism will work unless the operator has the necessary degree of extrasensory perception, and this is why it has been declared illegal to use such instruments for diagnosis in the United States. Our principal interest was in discovering the mechanism which produces the stickiness. Asked to watch the phenomenon, DVK observed that there was an increase of etheric energy at the fingertips, but that this emanated from the mental level, since without focused thought the sticky feeling does not occur. Apparently this type of extrasensory perception was activated by rubbing the fingers across an object.

Those clairvoyants, such as DVK, who are able to perceive the chakras within the etheric body, are using quite a different mechanism, however. In them the etheric brow chakra, in conjunction with the crown center, forms the organ of perception for etheric, astral and mental energies. Even among those who have well developed etheric sight, differences exist in the degree of clarity, precision and detail in their vision. It is difficult to find someone of DVK's ability who is at the same time willing to cooperate in time-consuming research that requires close attention and meticulous reporting. The clairvoyant has to focus and refocus constantly in order to report what is being observed. This is very strenuous, and three hours is the maximum time in which such work can be done efficiently without fatigue.

The mechanism of clairvoyant perception is as baffling to the seers as to the researchers. The use of their faculty is automatic to those so endowed, but without exception they find it very difficult to analyze, just as the ordinary sighted person would find it impossible to describe the mechanics of vision. However, continued observation of clairvoyants in the process of using their faculty has produced some interesting facts.

When SK observed DVK in the act of "turning on" her clairvoyance, a sudden change in the expression of the eyes became noticeable. The facial expression suggested an inward withdrawal of consciousness. Further study of this phenomenon led to an interesting neurological finding. The pupils of clairvoyants' eyes become slightly *dilated* and *fixed* for the whole period during which they are using this faculty. If a light is flashed in their eyes, their pupils do not constrict in the normal way.[2] But when the clairvoyants return to normal physical vision, their pupils immediately react with the light reflex, and contract normally. The seers have no control over this neurological reflex phenomenon, and are not aware of it. In fact, they were surprised when it was pointed out to them.

However, when seers concentrate upon their clairvoyant faculties, they retain full waking consciousness. Under test, they have invariably been able to describe accurately where their skin was touched lightly with cotton while they were in the clairvoyant state.

As explained, normal people were initially studied in order to establish a baseline for DVK's observations of the energy fields and their centers. Later, documented medical cases were evaluated. As the variety of diseases increased, so many more types of etheric energy fields were described, and the research method became more practiced and skillful.

In order to show some of the problems we encountered, and the difficulties the clairvoyant has in analyzing her own perceptions, we include a discussion between DVK and SK.

SK: How do you see the internal organs of the body?

DVK: I think I see two patterns, one of which is the energy pattern. I can tell at a glance whether there is a disharmony in this pattern, and it indicates to me where the disturbance is. Then I look at the disturbance in several ways. For example, I might look in detail at the chakra associated with that area. But at other times I might only

2. SK took a great many photographs of DVK's eyes during the times when she was using her clairvoyance, but unfortunately these were all lost following SK's sudden death.

look at the area that is disturbed. If I see a perturbation in the energy pattern, then I can, as it were, shift my focus and see the replica of the physical organs in the etheric body. How exact that replica is, or how exact my interpretation is, I do not know, but I think I can distinguish the things I am familiar with, such as blood and muscles.

SK: Is the blood different in color from the etheric, which you usually report appears grayish-blue?

DVK: That is the color of the etheric energy level. But when I look at an organ like the stomach in what I call "close focusing," I see the blood as red.

SK: Let us take a blood vessel. How would you see it on the etheric level, and would it be different in terms of the energy pattern?

DVK: The energy pattern is like lines of electricity within the grayish-blue etheric body, and it also has a rhythm. But a blood vessel looks like a clear glass or plastic tube, through which a reddish fluid is running.

SK: If you look at a vein on the dorsum [back] of my hand, how does it appear to you?

DVK: It looks like a channel running just under the skin, with a faint clear yellowish color.

SK: If you look at the veins of an elderly person who might have changes in the blood vessels, would they be different?

DVK: The channel would not be so tight and firm; it might be wider. The tone would be more "soggy," and there might be little particles in the flow, as well as small blockages. Material that appears a little "woody," I take to be cholesterol.

SK: Is this material whirling?

DVK: No. There is whirling on the energy level, but the level I am speaking of is a replica of the physical world. It is much harder to concentrate on these etheric details than it is to look at the energetic aspects, because in the latter case you can make snap judgments based on an overall picture, and these are pretty accurate.

SK: Which level of the etheric would the blood represent, in comparison with the general energy level?

DVK: Probably the lowest of the etheric. The energy is at a higher level.

SK: Can you describe how you see a stomach ulcer?

DVK: At the edge of the stomach there is blood. The ulcer creates material which affects both the stomach itself and the blood which flows through the stomach. Sometimes I can see a lot of blood leaking into the big sack of the stomach, which then looks very raw around its walls.

SK: How do you perceive the causes of the ulcer?

DVK: Ulcers result from emotional tension, but they also depend a great deal on individual temperament. One person can be extremely tense and yet have no stomach problem at all; he will never develop ulcers. My personal theory is that some people are born with certain etheric tendencies, as, for example, a weakness in the solar plexus. Such an individual will feel things very strongly, but he may try to suppress these emotions and remain calm. As a result, he builds up pressure in the digestive system and becomes more and more tense; this causes him to "thin out," as it were, etherically speaking, so that he does not take in enough energy. I have seen the beginnings of an ulcer when it was still in the baby stage, and watched it become bigger and bigger over a period of time.

SK: From your description, it appears that there is first a loss of vitality in the area—a blanching, so to speak, as though it was devitalized.

DVK: That's right; the tension begins first.

SK: What does a healing ulcer look like?

DVK: The color of the blood returns to normal, and the energy swings up.

SK: Can you actually see where the ulcer is?

DVK: I have been able to see an ulcerous condition which has not yet reached the hemorrhage stage. The blood vessels look loose, and they widen in the area of the incipient ulcer.

Following this dialogue, DVK was asked to observe some inanimate objects etherically, in order to discover whether what we call the nonliving has some degree of vitality. She had already made some observations of crystals and had seen that they have a small degree of etheric energy. She was handed a little piece of myrrh, and asked to compare it with the crystals. Without knowing quite what it was that she was holding in her hand, she reported as follows:

"This is not a crystal because it does not have sharp lines and angles of energy through it. It does seem to be growing, but the process is more like cell reproduction than crystalline growth. The growth is more on the surface than at the core; it seems to grow on something else, and to draw energy from that source. As a whole, it is more alive than a crystal, but not as clear-cut. When I hold the piece in my hand, I have more etheric interaction with it than in the case of a crystal, and that interaction is more pronounced in the palm of the hand than in the fingers. This substance feels more porous than a crystal, and in response to the warmth of my hand, it seems to take in more energy than it gives out."

Continuing her observation of crystals, DVK was asked to evaluate a cylindrical white crystal sent us by Dr. Puthoff of Stanford University. This crystal had been bombarded by some kind of energy, and Dr. Harold Puthoff wanted to know whether the pattern of the crystal had been changed. DVK's assessment was that the etheric energy field had been interfered with, and as a result the normal energy pattern had been fractured, so that the energy flow broke and went in a different direction. It flowed as though something had been done under pressure. This assessment was found to be correct.

According to DVK, there is a far greater interaction between crystals, gemstones and human energy than most people realize. The crystalline structure is somehow able to pick up, focus and retain etheric energy for long periods of time, but in such a way that it is accessible and can be used by people as a focus in sending out healing energy.

Such observations indicate that not only is there an etheric field associated with living matter, but also that all natural substances have a degree of vitality or "life." Our research did not take us very far in this direction, but it indicates the truth of V.A. Firsoff's statement, "We come here very close to the boundary line between life and non-life, if there is such a boundary. It may be no more than a matter of definition."[3]

3. V.A. Firsoff. *At the Crossroads of Knowledge.* Ian Henry Publications, Ltd., 1977.

4

Observations of the Disease Process

X

Variations in the Etheric Field

One of the primary aims of our research was to obtain a clear and precise description of the etheric body under normal healthy conditions, and to note the changes that take place when disease has set in or is imminent. It was of equal importance to observe, whenever possible, how healing is accomplished—whether spontaneously or with the aid of medications, healers or other therapeutic measures—and the changes effected thereby in vital functions.

Following a year of preliminary work, we developed an outline which listed all the characteristics of the etheric body that are of diagnostic importance.

The first of these is *color*: normally, pale violet or blue-gray.

The second is degree of *brightness*: this may vary from strongly luminous to dull, but should be uniform throughout.

The third is *motion*: movement should be rhythmic throughout the field, but may be fast, average or slow.

The fourth is *form*: size, shape and symmetry are all important.

The fifth is *angle*: the etheric should stand out at right angles to the physical body; if it is droopy in part or as a whole, this indicates ill health.

The sixth is *elasticity*: the ability of the etheric to stretch and expand is a sign of health.

The seventh is *texture*: the quality should be firm and fairly fine; if it is coarse, porous, spongy, thin or broken, it should be noted whether this condition is generalized or limited to a section of the etheric field, for this indicates some kind of illness or abnormality.

All of these characteristics offer clues to the general state of health and indicate where we should expect physical problems to arise, and whether they will manifest soon or later in life.

Finally, we looked for the general *function* of the etheric field as a whole, that is, the quality of the interactions within the chakra system as a whole, as well as the energy flow throughout the etheric body.

For purposes of comparison, we established a norm against which we tested each patient:

The average, healthy etheric body should have the following characteristics:

Color	-	pale violet-gray
Luminosity	-	moderate
Texture	-	firm and fairly fine
Elasticity	-	moderate
Form	-	symmetrical
Rhythm	-	rhythmic and moderate in speed

Special Indicators

Certain features of the etheric have, in DVK's experience, become indicators of malfunctioning or evidence of a disease process. When the outline of the etheric body is fairly stable and not dented or broken, this is an indication of health. If a person is ill, the outline of the etheric body becomes uneven and the normal energy flow through the chakras is reduced. This affects the energy flow of the different physical organs involved in the disease process.

When the energy pattern is closely knit, it is very resistant to invasion from the outside world, but when loose and porous it can be penetrated more easily, and therefore the subject is apt to take in whatever may be in the surrounding environment. In DVK's opinion, vaccinations or infections for which we develop immunity produce variations in the cycle of the energy flow pattern, slight as these may be.

The blood flow and the lymphatic system are also important. Looked at clairvoyantly, the lymphatic system appears spongy and loosely woven. Etherically, the lymph seems to have a minus charge, while the blood has a plus charge. This conclusion was based on the observation that the blood had more "sparks" of etheric energy than the lymph, which appeared paler, slightly grayish in color, and less vigorous. The lymph seemed to be receptive in its interaction with the blood stream, as unwanted products in the blood were transferred to the lymph glands, which were perceived as holding points for certain energies rejected by the blood.

The lymphatic system seems to balance the energy of the etheric body by controlling the amount of blood flowing to any one area.

Variations in the Etheric Due to Paranormal Abilities

In individuals who have some higher sense perception, especially telepathy, the etheric seems to be finer in texture than in the average person, and also slightly larger and more rhythmic.

In the case of healers, the appearance of the etheric field varies. The majority of those who use their hands during healing are to some degree using part of their own etheric field to help the patient, though energies from the universal field also come into play. As a result, their etheric fields seem to have more elasticity than the average, thus enabling them to transmit energy to the patient. An exception to this practice was the case of the well-known healer, Katherine Kuhlman, (see Chapter XVI) who transmitted a type of energy which was not directly related to her own etheric field. She acted somewhat like a lightning rod, in that she was the agency through which etheric and/or astral energies in the general field were activated and transmitted. In the case of exceptional healers, such as Miss Kuhlman, there are other factors which come into play, and these will be discussed more fully in Chapter XVI.

In a trance-medium, the etheric varies from the norm in several ways. If the medium goes into a trance frequently over a long period of time, certain changes take place. The texture of the etheric becomes increasingly spongy and porous, and its connection with the physical body loosens. Physical problems related to the kidneys, adrenals and water metabolism may arise from these etheric changes and abnormalities manifest themselves through fluctuations in body weight. In many cases of trance-mediumship the physical body type is heavy and retains fluids. Repetitive trance states also induce a loosening of the astral and mental fields from the etheric/physical. By breathing over-rapidly, the medium may sometimes exit from the body, not in the normal manner via the crown chakra, but via the solar plexus. This separates the etheric from the astral and mental fields, and prevents the medium from recalling what took place during the trance. It also accounts for the fatigue and exhaustion that follow.

Observations of a Medium During Trance

In 1958 we observed B. Mc., who had been a professional trance-medium for many years. Her etheric field had the following characteristics: The color was misty, grayer than average, and murky. It was of average brightness and rhythm, but the rate of movement was slow, increasing during the trance state. Her etheric was slightly larger than the average, extending beyond the physical body. Instead of the lines of energy being erect, it was droopy, and there seemed to be a depression on the left side of the head. The elasticity was excellent, but the texture was porous and spongy, and it was broken and segmented over the solar plexus area. This looseness and porosity were the most marked etheric characteristics.

DVK observed B. Mc. both before and during the trance state. Just before she went into the trance and became unconscious, her solar plexus center began to vibrate, and at this point she took energy from the corresponding chakras of those present for whom she was giving the "reading," thus establishing the contact.

As she opened herself to the astral consciousness, her whole etheric became limp and droopy. Her breathing became rapid, which affected the brain, and she let herself lose conscious control of her body. As the core of her crown center opened and became more elastic, she herself became open to astral consciousnesses. This process took a few minutes, during which a degree of harmony and coordination was established between herself and the pulse of this new astral energy.

Shortly after this, B. Mc. went into a full trance state and exited from her body. Her consciousness became completely quiescent when full harmony was established with the astral consciousness. Its rhythm was superimposed on hers, thus enabling it to use part of her brain mechanism, which changed at the moment she entered the trance state. The etheric brain pattern speeded up, yet at the same time dulled. Thus she became a focus for other influences, and spoke aloud and gave messages in an altered voice. During trance, both the crown and the solar plexus centers speeded up. The core of the throat center, like that of the solar plexus, opened and became wider. The core of the solar plexus, however, was the one most affected: as it became wider, it became more elastic and dysrhythmic, and this condition increased throughout the trance state. Also the reddish color of the chakra was accentuated.

B. Mc's solar plexus center was the most developed of all her chakras, which made her sensitive to the feelings of other people, but at the same time had a deleterious effect on her adrenal glands.

This case has been included because it is fairly characteristic of the phenomenon of trance-mediumship. In such a case, the physical senses become dulled; the person is commonly not aware of what is taking place, and does not remember what has been said. The consciousness is fully focused on another level.

Today there are many people who are open to impressions of the emotional or astral level. However, this kind of sensitivity is not in the same class as that of trance-mediumship, which is a fairly rare phenomenon that usually develops quite early in life.

XI

The Chakras and the
Endocrine Glands

During the course of our research into the role of the chakras in health and disease, over 200 cases were observed clairvoyantly, and in a large number of these the disease was found to be related to the endocrine glands (see pullout inside the back cover). In a small group of subjects, the astral as well as the etheric chakras were studied, and in a very few subjects, the mental chakras were added.

We were fortunate to be able to keep contact with a few of the subjects over a period of time—in some cases, for many years. In those that received extensive follow-up (over twenty-five years), it was possible to verify DVK's initial diagnosis of abnormalities through a subsequent onset of the indicated disease. In our present limited state of knowledge of the whole field of clairvoyant investigation, we do not know if it might be possible to modify an abnormal condition observed in the etheric centers before the disease manifests itself, and thus remove its causes.

Studies of the etheric chakras showed that whenever there were severe abnormalities in their colors, rhythm, direction of movement, brightness, form, elasticity and texture, this indicated a serious condition, probably resulting in the development of a disease, either in the endocrine glands related to that center or in that part of the body to which the center provides energy.

The Chakra System

Name	Color	Location	Gland
Crown	Gold core Violet/gold petals	Above the head	Pineal
Brow	Rose/yellow Blue/purple	Between the eyes	Pituitary
Throat	Silvery blue	Base of neck	Thyroid/ Parathyroid
Heart	Golden yellow	Midway between shoulder blades	Thymus
Solar plexus	Many-colored: red and green	Navel	Adrenals/ pancreas
Root	Orange-red	Base of spine	Spine/ Glandular system

Lesser Chakras

Name	Color	Location	Gland
Spleen	Many-colored: yellow, rose-red predominating	Left of abdomen, below 10th rib	Spleen/ Liver
Sacral	Vermilion red	Genital/spinal region	Ovaries/ testicles

Subsidiary Chakras

Palms of hands - Soles of feet

Note: See pullout inside the back cover of this book for illustrations of the major chakras. The panel showing individual chakras can be unfolded so that it is visible while one is reading the book.

The harmonics of the chakras in the etheric, astral and mental fields is an important factor, for dissonance can give rise to disease in that part of the body which the center serves. Studies of a chakra made on the three levels have established some information regarding the harmonics of the chakra system. For example, if we assume that the speed of the etheric center is one, then the astral center's speed of rotation should be double and the mental center's four times that rate, i.e., a ratio of 1:2:4. In actuality, of course, the rates are much higher, but this ratio would indicate that the chakras are working together harmoniously. If, on the other hand, the rate of an astral center is higher than that of the mental, as for example 1:5:3, the possibility of dissonance and disease associated with that astral center is indicated. In any case, it shows that the patient's emotions, not his mind, control his physical responses.

It is worth noting that some physicians today advocate visualization to help patients overcome the effects of certain diseases, such as cancer, which may originate at the emotional level—although the etiology of cancer is complex, and many causative factors come into play. If visualization is beneficial, it may be because it increases the flow of mental energy and balances and calms the emotions.

Our observations showed that when changes occurred in the centers in the form of dysrhythmia, especially if there was a reversal of the movement from clockwise to counterclockwise, the potential for disease was very marked. If this was accompanied by other changes, whether in color, degree of brightness, form or texture, the malfunctioning was exaggerated. In addition, if the core of the center displayed a conflicting dual movement, that is, turning both clockwise and counterclockwise, within a few years the patient was likely to develop a growth, probably cancerous, related to those parts of the body supplied by that center. This opinion is based on a number of cases where the observations were made years before the onset of disease.

In severe physical abnormalities, where the glands related to the chakra had been surgically excised, it was noted that the surgery did not correct the abnormality in the center itself. The persistence of this abnormal condition may help explain the recurrence of the disease in the organs of the body that were partially excised, such as the thyroid.

A brief extract from the discussions which led to our categorization of abnormalities in the chakras may be of interest:

SK: How do you perceive a "crack," or leak, in an etheric center?

DVK: Every time the center, during its rotation, comes to the place where the leak is, this produces a confusion in the rhythm. It is as if the energy is disturbed as it passes through into the body.

SK: What do you perceive if there is a slight leak in a center?

DVK: There will be a corresponding disturbance in the rhythm, but not necessarily a disalignment.

SK: What do you mean when you say there is good alignment in the chakras?

DVK: If there is good alignment there is usually no disturbance in the rhythm or color. But if there is a disturbance, I look for dysrhythmia or disalignment. If the rhythm and color are within the normal range, there is no disalignment, although the chakras may not be quite in harmony.

At present we are learning which parts of the body are energized and therefore controlled by the different chakras, but we do not as yet know what factors determine exactly where disease will show itself when an abnormality develops in a center. For example, if the etheric throat chakra shows some abnormality in color, such as the presence of red in the core or petals, we do not know whether this indicates that disease will appear in the thyroid gland itself, or whether the breast or the chest will be affected. All of these areas are energized by the throat center. Likewise, we do not yet know whether the malfunction will be hormonal, or whether it may lead to a growth, either benign or cancerous. On the other hand, no disease related to an etheric chakra was ever found when the center itself was perceived to be absolutely normal.

Another observation that has long-range implications is that genetic defects show up in the chakras.

All of these clues lead us to hope that in the future new techniques will be developed which are capable of detecting the behavior of the etheric chakras, so that abnormalities can be discovered before physical symptoms appear. This would be an enormous stride in the direction of real preventive medicine. This idea may seem far-fetched at present, but it is only by looking at the origin of disease that we can hope to find its means of prevention.

Persistent abnormalities in the centers may be analogous to the incubation period which exists in infectious diseases. We know that in certain of these the incubation periods vary from three to seven or from fourteen to twenty-one days. One question to consider is: What are the determining factors between the time of infection and the onset of symptoms of the disease? A second question is: Why do we have a specific set of symptoms which are characteristic for every disease?

The answers to these and other puzzling questions may lie in the harmonics of the chakra system.

Every comment and conclusion we make in this book is based upon experimental evidence drawn from case histories in which the disease process showed itself in anomalies both in the field(s) and in the chakras. Some of our readers may wish to study this evidence for themselves; others may find it tedious and prefer that we extrapolate. Therefore, our text is followed by an appendix in which detailed case histories are given in full, but in the narrative itself we generalize for the reader to the extent that we feel is warranted.

However, if these generalizations are to be meaningful, the reader should know how we arrived at them, and for this, the correspondences between the individual chakras and the various endocrine glands need to be identified. The case histories in the appendix which are most closely related to each particular chakra are indicated. Because the chakras all interact with one another, however, in some instances more complete information about the whole chakra system is needed; in such cases the data is more detailed and includes a description of other chakras and/or the whole field; in a few cases the astral chakras are also described.

It should be reemphasized that DVK did not know the medical diagnosis prior to her observation of the patients, except in those cases where there was a return visit.

The Crown Chakra

As noted in Chapter V, the crown chakra is the largest and most important center. It affects the function of the whole brain, but is especially related to the pineal gland. Because of its interconnections with the other chakras, any disturbance in the crown center is reflected in most of the centers.

The pineal gland is a reddish-gray body, the size of a pea and the shape of a pine cone; hence its name. It lies deep in the brain (above and behind the posterior commissure, between the anterior corpora quadrigemina, on which it rests, and beneath the posterior border of the corpus callosum).

For a long time, the pineal was considered to be a vestigial organ without function or use. However, in the seventeenth century the philosopher Descartes stated that the pineal was the seat of the soul and the only place where mind and body interact, because everywhere else they are hopelessly sundered, being (so he argued) of two entirely different substances. His writings also implied that the eyes might play a role in the mechanism. Many people ridiculed his statements, but today, 300 years later, the pineal gland is being actively investigated by medical scientists, even if his uncompromising dualism is rejected in favor of a more unified view of reality.

In 1959 there was a major breakthrough in understanding the function of this gland, when Lerner, a dermatologist, succeeded in isolating the hormone melatonin, produced by the pineal. It was found that the production of melatonin was high during the hours of the night and low during the day; this circadian rhythm is important in terms of the body's biological clocks. Similar compounds were discovered in the retina of the eye.

Contemporary research confirms that the pineal gland produces hormones which control other biological rhythms, and that it has several endocrine connections. In 1960, Kappers discovered that the primary nerves that serve the pineal originate not within the brain, but rather in the sympathetic nervous system (specifically in sympathetic cell bodies in the superior cervical ganglia). (cf. *The New Scientist*, July 25, 1985, and *Science News*, November 9, 1985.)

Diseases Related to the Crown Chakra

Of the many cases studied which were specifically related to abnormalities in the crown chakra, we have selected that of CT, a Methodist minister and healer, aged seventy-five, who developed paralysis of the right side of the body with difficulty in speaking (aphasia and apraxia) on July 5, 1958. Some improvement had taken place when he was seen in April, 1959. (See pp. 200-235 of the appendix for full details.)

Observation of his general field showed that the etheric had patches of gray scattered throughout, with darker shades of gray around the head. The luminosity was above average, but there were dull spots within the field. There was both a rhythmic and dysrhythmic pattern to the movement, in that it was slower around the head, where there was also poor elasticity. Moreover, the etheric was droopy on the right side of the head and broken into fine granules on the left side, which indicated damage to the brain. The etheric fingers of the right hand were elongated, showing a potential for healing.

SK's comment on these observations, after consulting the medical diagnosis, was that the correlation between DVK's description and the medical condition was excellent. The basic damage was assessed by the granulation of the etheric on the left side of the brain, and the droopiness on the right side coincided with the paralysis.

The crown chakra was abnormal, with a large discrepancy between the color, luminosity, rate of motion, elasticity and texture of the core and those of the petals. Whereas the luminosity of the petals gave evidence of the practice of meditation, the dullness of the core indicated a disease process. DVK's description of what she perceived etherically in the brain was interesting. She stated that the part of the brain which seems to deal with the mechanism of hearing is what she thinks of as the "sounding board." The electrical impulses which normally act as this sounding board were damaged in this case, and this in turn interfered with the mechanism of hearing. The "monitor of speech" within the etheric brain was missing. There was also dysrhythmia, with a slowing of energy in the frontal lobes. The energy in the posterior part of the brain was jagged, as compared to the frontal lobes. SK hypothesized that the area of decreased energy on the left side above the core of the chakra was probably due to the damage on the left side of the brain.

Another disease which is especially related to the crown center is epilepsy. We saw a considerable number of such cases, of which we give one representative account. (Additional material will be found in the appendix.)

MJ, twenty-one years of age, had bilaterial EEG abnormalities, with one side showing more disturbance than the other. She was first seen by Dr. Wilder Penfield at the Montreal Neurological Institute in 1952, having suffered from epileptic seizures since early childhood. The warning signals, called the "aura," were a sensation in the head, palpitations, staring, movements of mastication, and automatic rather than spontaneous actions. These minor seizures were sometimes, but not always, followed by a major seizure with loss of consciousness.

MJ had a large birthmark on the right side of her face, forehead and scalp. Her behavior was unpredictable and at times dangerous. She periodically exhibited violent temper, jealousy and aggressive behavior; she would slap her mother, throw things around and break objects. She demanded constant attention and was very strong-willed.

The medical report indicated evidence of brain damage (independent epileptiform disturbance from the left temporal region, though the maximum discharge was clearly right-sided). Dr. Penfield performed two surgical excisions on the right rear portion of the brain, (a right posterio-temporal lobectomy), one in 1952 and the second in 1953. There was a 75 percent improvement in her seizures and behavior, but her jealousy and temper tantrums remained.

DVK saw the patient in New York City in 1957. She had no knowledge whatsoever of the medical history, nor did she receive any information about the patient.

She reported that the general etheric field was unbalanced on the sides of the head. On the left side, the etheric was pushed inward; the right side of the head as well as the body extended about two centimeters farther out. The texture of the right side seemed thicker, penetrating about three centimeters deeper into the etheric brain. In addition, the energy seemed jerky in the right prefrontal lobe as compared with the left.

The color in this area of the etheric was dark gray, mixed with some dark red, which is not normal. The texture was slightly coarse and the movement was erratic, with a crisscross flow. The very substance of the etheric brain seemed to be disharmonious; the energy flow was unstable and jerky in the prefrontal lobes.

In the region back of the right eye, deep within the substance of the brain, there were "jumps" in the energy pattern. On the right side of the brain there was a "bare patch," where the etheric energy seemed to jump across an empty space. (DVK pointed to the right temporal and right precentral region when making this observation, which coincided with the part of the brain on that side that had been removed surgically.) She saw the area of disturbance of the precentral region as "a long, narrow, ditch-like channel," where the etheric flow was abnormal.

The crown chakra was about fifteen centimeters in width, and about three centimeters above the top of the head. The petals on the right side, located at around six and eight o'clock, were pointing downward, which is abnormal, and they also showed some abnormal bare patches. The core of the crown center was about two-and-a-half centimeters across, elongated, dilated, wider and more elastic than normal, and the pattern of energy in this chakra seemed complex.

A definite disturbance was perceived in the crown chakra, indicating that the patient was subject to changes in consciousness which might lead to partial or complete unconsciousness. The stem of the crown center dipped in front, and seemed to produce pressure on some of the nerve centers. This in turn affected her sense perception, and therefore her responses appeared erratic. The right side seemed to have short and jerky wave patterns, while the left side had longer patterns.

DVK remarked that if the patient were to get emotionally upset or tired, the etheric energy would be short-circuited, and therefore her responses would become more erratic, her sense of balance lost, and she would become confused.

The etheric brow chakra was about seven centimeters wide and extended one centimeter in front of the forehead. Its movement was very slow, and this affected the prefrontal lobe region of the brain.

The throat chakra was about four centimeters wide, located about one centimeter from the front of the neck. It showed that the subject had undergone a lot of tension for a long period, which made her feel shut in and constricted, and this in turn produced more inner tension and slowed the flow of etheric energy. DVK noticed, however, that there was a definite improvement over the condition she must have been in previously. This was medically correct.

The patient was seen again in February 1958. At that time DVK observed that there were still zigzag energy patterns inside the brain around the seven and nine o'clock regions. The petals of the crown chakra showed some improvement, and were less downward-pointing. DVK remarked that the patient would at times have a surplus of energy building up within her without any outlet. Therefore, the slightest emotional disturbance would break the jam and she would let go furiously. DVK suggested that if a constructive outlet for her emotional expression could be found, especially something rhythmic like music, dancing or folk singing, this would help release the inner tension.

Because the crown chakra was elastic and wider than normal, the patient would be open to influences of an undesirable nature, especially during periods of erratic behavior.

DVK's interpretation and comments about what she perceived in the crown chakra and the left side of the etheric brain related accurately to the results of surgical excision of parts of the brain. Her description of the patient's emotional disturbance and violent episodes was remarkably accurate.

The Brow Chakra

The brow chakra is especially related to the pituitary gland. This is a small reddish-gray vascular mass, oval in shape, weighing about one gram, 1.2 by 1.5 centimeters in size. It is located within a bony structure (called the sella turcica) in the base of the skull, about six centimeters or two inches from a point between the eyebrows. The gland is attached (by the infundibulum) to the under-surface of the brain (the hypothalamus). Anatomically and functionally, it is composed of two lobes, separated from each other by a fibrous plate or lamina. The front or anterior portion is larger and has an oblong form, some-what concave behind, where it receives the round lobe behind it (posterior lobe). These two lobes differ in their development, structure and hormonal secretion.

The anterior lobe is dark reddish-brown in color, and resembles the thyroid in its microscopic structure. (It has been developed embryologically from the epiblast of the buccal cavity.) The anterior pituitary hormones are regulated by the hypothalamus (by neurohormones elaborated by neurosecretory cells.) The anterior pituitary gland secretes the following hormones, which in turn regulate the other glands in the body:

Corticotropin (ACTH), affecting the adrenal cortex
Thyroid stimulating hormone (TSH)

Follicle stimulating hormone in females (FSH)
Luteinizing hormone (LH)
Growth hormone (GH)
Lactogenic hormone called Prolactin (PRL)

The posterior lobe is developed as an outgrowth of the embryonic brain. (It becomes fused to the anterior pituitary lobe in mammalians.) It produces the following hormones:

Antidiuretic hormone (ADH) which stimulates
    water reabsorption by the kidneys
Oxytocin, which helps in the contraction of
    the pregnant uterus and releases milk
    by the lactating breast

Diseases Related to the Brow Chakra

Since the pituitary gland governs the hormones of the other endocrine glands, the medical profession assumed that surgical excision of the pituitary might delay or inhibit the growth of the metastases of cancer to other parts of the body. In nine cases of severe disorders of the pituitary gland studied at the New York Outpatient Center, seven had had surgical excision of the gland for therapeutic purposes. No outward physical signs were present. In five cases, the surgical excision was made in patients who had cancer of the breast with metasteses. In two cases, the excision was made for metabolic disturbances (Hans-Schuller-Christian disease and Paget's disease).

In all of these nine cases, DVK observed that the etheric brow chakras showed definite abnormalities. In seven of the cases, she described an absence of etheric energy in the core of the pituitary gland, a plausible observation since the gland had been surgically removed. In two cases of very rare diseases of the bones, she accurately described the changes in the bone structure, although these were diametrically different from one another. In no case did she perceive a diseased pituitary gland to be normal.

Initially, DVK was not aware that it was ever possible

to remove the pituitary gland surgically, but her observation of the etheric counterpart was accurate: she perceived it to be dull and without energy. Surgery in that area of the brain is not an easy procedure, and the pituitary gland might not have been removed completely, but she reported that the central portion was missing. In a few cases where the surgical excision was presumably incomplete, she reported slight amounts of etheric energy in the periphery of the pituitary gland. In no case, however, was the etheric brow chakra restored to normalcy after the pituitary was removed.

A case particularly related to abnormalities in the brow chakra is that of a woman suffering from diabetes insipidus, which involves the pituitary, and whose symptoms are excessive thirst and urine excretion. The patient is usually nervous, jittery and apprehensive, and in this case she suffered severe headaches on the right side, extending to the forehead. These occurred six months after the birth of a child. Subsequently, she developed Hans-Schuller-Christian disease, a metabolic disturbance, for which she received X-ray treatment as well as medication.

DVK observed that the etheric brow chakra was severely abnormal, as evidenced by a gray color in both petals and core, irregularity in the core as well as some leakage, and a general thickness and looseness of the etheric material. The periphery of the etheric pituitary gland was softer and more elastic than normal, and its activity was irregular: the center and right side of the gland were more active than the other parts. The bones on the top of the head (in the region of the fontanelle) seemed harder than normal and also thicker, but not uniformly so. They were also less elastic.

In this case DVK's observations corresponded accurately with the medical findings, especially with respect to her description of the quality of the bones.

(Details of this and other cases related to the brow chakra are to be found in the appendix.)

The Throat Chakra

The throat chakra is most closely linked with the thyroid

and parathyroid glands. The thyroid gland is of supreme importance to the well-being of the average individual, for it controls metabolic rate and balances body equilibrium. There is a close relationship between the parathyroid and the two lobes of the thyroid gland.

The thyroid gland weighs 30 grams and is located in the neck just below the larynx or "voice box." One of its functions is to increase oxygen consumption, and thus it regulates the processes of growth and tissue differentiation. The gland produces the thyroid hormone for controlling metabolism, and calcitonin, which helps in the decrease of blood calcium. The thyroid gland is essential for normal functioning, as it increases protein synthesis in virtually every body tissue.

The parathyroid glands are four or five small round bodies, each about the size of a lentil, attached to the posterior surface of the lobes of the thyroid gland. Their chief function is to maintain the homeostasis of blood calcium, which they do by stimulating the breakdown of bones, thus releasing calcium and phosphate into the bloodstream. They also increase blood calcium by stimulating its absorption from the intestines and kidney tubules.

The principal regulators of calcium and phosphorous homeostasis in the body are the parathyroid hormone and Vitamin D. (Today, Vitamin D is considered to be a hormone.) In hyperparathyroidism, there is a generalized disorder of calcium phosphate and bone metabolism, resulting from an increased secretion of the parathyroid hormone by the parathyroid glands, giving rise to hypercalcemia.

Various types of dysrhythmia have been observed in the throat center. More people show some disturbance in this area than in any other etheric chakra. If the chakra is "droopy" and its rhythm is slowed, this indicates a general debility and a tendency to fatigue; in states of tension, however, the core becomes tighter while the petals become looser, and the energy is dysrhythmic. Occasionally a break is perceived in the rhythm, much like a crack in a record, and this indicates a slight leakage of energy. In some mental disorders, the throat chakra may show a tear.

Diseases Related to the Throat Chakra

Numerous cases of normal and slightly deviated etheric throat centers were studied. In twelve cases of cancer where the thyroid gland had been removed surgically, DVK observed that the etheric gland was missing. In those cases in which there had been a partial resection, she reported that part of the thyroid had been removed. In all the cases observed, the throat chakra remained abnormal even after surgical excision of the cancerous growth. The time it would take to regain normality after surgery is an interesting subject for research.

In one case of particular interest, the patient (RS) was suffering from Paget's disease, which involves a chronic inflammation of the bones, especially the pelvis, femur, vertebrae and skull, whose size also changes. (See the appendix under brow chakra for full details.) DVK observed that the function of the throat chakra was abnormal, especially in the vortex, which had slowed down. The thyroid gland looked "dead," and had probably been removed, and the parathyroids were not functioning normally. The low intensity of energy in these glands, which seemed to be flickering and out of balance with the thyroid, led her to surmise that the patient had a disease of the parathyroids. (The medical history showed that the right parathyroid had been excised for adenoma, and she had had a left hemithyroidectomy.)

On the right side of the skull the bone seemed to be "thinned out," a condition repeated to a lesser degree in the back of the head and in the bones of the spine and legs. In normal bones the etheric texture looks hard and thick, but in this patient the structure of the bones looked "crumbly" and in small pieces. (This was strikingly different from the bone condition observed in the previous case of diabetes insipidus.) The bone structure was particularly thin and granular on the right side of the head.

Observing the organs, DVK felt that the adrenals were hypofunctioning and that the liver was sluggish. The left kidney seemed normal, but there was some indication of a soft stone. The right kidney was not functioning normally, and displayed the same "crumbly" appearance, as did the intestinal tract. There was an unusual gray color present in the core of the solar plexus chakra, which was both slow and dysrhythmic in its function.

In this case, DVK's observations correlated extremely well with the medical diagnosis, especially with respect to the condition of the bones.

The Heart Chakra

The heart center is closely linked with the physical heart, the blood stream and its circulation, and the electrical balance of the lymphatic system. It is connected with the thymus gland and, according to present information, with the immune system.

The thymus gland consists of two lateral lobes held in close contact by a connective tissue, and it is encapsulated. It is found along the midline of the chest, (partly in the neck and partly in the superior mediastinum, extending from the fourth costal cartilage upward as high as the lower border of the thyroid gland). Below, it rests on the heart (pericardium).

The thymus is pinkish-gray in color, soft and lobulated on the surface. It is five centimeters in length and about three-and-a-half centimeters in breadth. At birth it weighs about eight grams, but it diminishes in the adult and is scarcely recognizable in advanced age. It was formerly considered a vestigial gland and of little importance; at one time it was believed to function simply as a producer of lymph cells (lymphocytes).

Since 1960, however, the thymus has been recognized to be of great importance in the maturation of a competent immunological system. Its essential hormone is thymosin (an active peptide), which helps in the development of the immune system, and the thymus is therefore key to the ability to produce antibodies and to reject foreign tissues and cells.

Early in 1959, when DVK was presented with many subjects and asked to evaluate their etheric centers and corresponding endocrine glands, her first unexpected observation was that the thymus gland deals with the immunity of the body. This was unknown to the medical profession at the time, for it was not until later in the 1960s that the finding was reported in medical journals.

DVK observed that the etheric thymus gland appears firmer, brighter and less spongy in children than in adults, and that it has more energy. During exercise, a child's thymus has more effect on circulation than it does in an adult. This effect was observed to be more apparent in the lower portion of the thymus than the upper.

There is a bridge between the upper part of the thymus and the thyroid. If a person becomes emotionally disturbed, it is noticeable in the etheric connections between the thymus and the brain in the region of the pituitary gland. The lymph glands appear etherically to be more tightly knit as compared with the thymus, which seems loose and spongy.

Physically, the heart chakra seems principally to affect the operation of the valves of the heart. In adults, the rhythm of the heart is conditioned by the pacemaker. DVK observed that there might be some connection between heart rhythm and emotional states, which affect the thymus. Heart rhythm is also connected with the effects of meditation upon the astral heart chakra.

Diseases Related to the Heart Chakra

MT, aged 76, had had a very enlarged heart for ten years, with no symptoms of heart failure, no swelling of the feet, no breathlessness. The subject had been very active.

In August, 1985, it was decided to tap the pericardium, from which 300 cc of fluid were aspirated. Although the fluid was clear and the bacteriological tests were negative, the patient was given an anti-inflammatory drug for two weeks. X-rays taken six weeks later showed that the improvement seen immediately after the aspiration from the pericardium remained constant.

In September, 1985, DVK observed the patient's heart chakra. The color was golden, but with some fluctuation; the rate showed some dysrhythmia and fluctuation; the texture was fairly coarse; the form showed a slight thinning at the periphery of the chakra.

Looking at the heart, DVK reported that there was a slight enlargement, which was normal for the subject. In addition, there was thickening of the pericardial membrane posteriorly, which probably had been present for a long time, and might have been a congenital anomaly. There did not seem to be an inflammatory condition, and there was no evidence of infection.

DVK's impression was that the heart was larger than the average, and that its pericardial membrane was too tight a fit. The resulting friction between the heart and the membrane during contraction produced the increased amount of fluid in the pericardial cavity.

The general level of vitality of the etheric was very good.

In this case the correlation between DVK's observation and the medical diagnosis was good.

The Solar Plexus Chakra

The solar plexus center is related to the *adrenal glands*, as well as to the pancreas, the liver and the area of the stomach.

The word "adrenal" means near or upon the kidney, and the glands so named are two triangular bodies covering the superior or upper surface of the kidneys. Each part of the double organ is composed of an outer layer or cortex and inner area or medulla. (Embryologically, the cortex arises from the mesoderm, which also gives rise to the gonads, and the medulla from the ectoderm, which gives rise to the sympathetic nervous system.) The entire gland is enclosed in a tough connective tissue from which bundles of fibers (trabeculae) extend into the cortex. The adrenals are three to five centimeters long and four to six millimeters in thickness, with an average weight of five grams.

The cortex secretes hormones that are synthesized from cholesterol. These are:

> *Glucocorticoids*, which deal with carbohydrate metabolism.
>
> *Mineralocorticoids*, which affect the metabolism of sodium and potassium.

Androgens, which consist of seventeen ketosteroids, estrogen and progestines, important in the physiology of reproduction, also in carbohydrate, water, muscle, bone, central nervous system, gastrointestinal, cardiovascular and hemotological metabolism. They are also anti-inflammatory agents.

The cortex may be considered the source of life-giving hormones. In adrenal hypofunction we have Addison's disease, which produces atrophy of the adrenal cortex with a decrease of blood sodium and chloride, and an increase in potassium, producing hypotension and circulatory collapse, fatal if untreated.

In 1932 the American neurosurgeon, Harvey Cushing, described a syndrome to which his name has been given. It results from hypersecretion of the adrenal cortex, and is characterized by obesity, hypertension, easy fatigability, weakness, hirsutism, edema, glucosuria and osteoporosis. There is excessive production of glucocorticoids. The disease may be caused by a tumor of the adrenal gland or excessive stimulation of that gland as a result of hyperfunction of the anterior pituitary.

The adrenal medulla synthesizes and stores dopamine, norepinephrine and epinephrine (adrenaline), and is connected with the sympathetic nervous system, producing effects in emotional states.

Diseases Related to the Solar Plexus Chakra

It is well known that stomach ulcers are strongly related to emotional stress, and this susceptibility is very evident in the solar plexus, which clearly registers personal emotional disturbances. There are close connections between this chakra and its astral counterpart, as well as with the whole emotional field, and observations have shown that when there are disturbances in the etheric solar plexus chakra, the astral is usually also involved.

A very interesting case involving the solar plexus chakra was that of DT, a well-known journalist and public speaker, a woman whose husband had died a few months before our interview. At this time there was no medical diagnosis, as the patient had not consulted a physician recently.

In observing the general etheric, DVK noted that there were color changes around the abdomen, above average luminosity, and dysrhythmia in that the rate of motion varied from fast to slow. The etheric was wider on the left side of the body, and it was droopy, with a split over the head area.

Looking at the abdomen and the internal organs, DVK described a blockage in the left upper region of the abdomen (near the splenic flexure), which she identified by pointing to the area. The subject had not complained of any gastrointestinal symptoms nor indicated any malady, and as mentioned above, she had not been medically evaluated.

The color of the petals of the solar plexus chakra was a pinkish-yellow, and from this DVK deduced that the patient was a person with very strong emotions, which she controlled and checked with her mind and will. She at times inhibited her personal feelings if she felt this was the right thing to do. This placed her adrenals under constant stress, and in addition she continually pushed herself to work at a pace which was really beyond her physical capacity.

After her evaluation, DVK recommended that the patient consult her physician and undergo an X-ray examination. The result of these tests showed a blockage of the colon exactly at the point DVK had indicated. Three days later, cancer of the descending colon was diagnosed and removed surgically.

As a followup, the patient was seen again a few weeks after surgery. DVK observed that the general etheric was less droopy but had not returned to normalcy. The blockage was gone, but the adrenals were still under stress.

In this case, the correlation between the clairvoyant observation and the medical findings was exact, but the observation preceded the diagnosis.

The Spleen Chakra

The spleen is an elongated, dark red ovoid body, lying in the upper left quadrant of the abdomen, behind and below the stomach.

One of the spleen's main functions is to resist infection. It is the site of specific antibody production ("B" cells), and serves to clear micro-organisms and cell debris from the plasma, thus functioning as an immunologic filter of the circulatory system. It is composed of two parts: the "white pulp" and the "red pulp." The functions of the white pulp are the generation of antibodies, the production of a hormone called "tuftsin," and also the maturation of "B" and "T" lymphocytes and plasma cells, which play a part in immunity. The functions of the red pulp are: the removal of unwanted particulate matter, such as bacteria or aging blood elements; the reservoir function of blood elements, leukocytes and platelets; a culling and pitting which removes inclusion bodies.

The spleen chakra provides one of the three most important points of entry into the body for etheric energy (prana), the other two being the lungs and the skin. DVK believes that blood formation is determined to a large extent by the width and degree of flow of etheric energy between the splenic chakra and the solar plexus chakra.

Diseases Related to the Spleen Chakra

If the spleen is removed surgically, the appearance of the spleen chakra seems to be unaffected, for it remains as visible and active as the others. Its physical functions related to blood formation and the storage of iron, in contrast to the processing of etheric energy, are transferred to the liver. (It should be noted that this does not correspond to the present medical view.)

However, a patient whose spleen was injured accidentally during abdominal surgery was observed a year later. The amount of etheric energy in the chakra was normal, but the center was slower than usual in absorbing and distributing the energy. In other words, it took longer for the center to recharge its vitality.

As mentioned in Chapter V, the spleen chakra has strong interconnections with all the other chakras, which it furnishes with additional prana or etheric energy from the universal field. In the case of a patient who suffered from chronic lymphatic leukemia, whose spleen and liver were enlarged, and whose thyroid had a nodule in it, DVK observed abnormalities in the throat, solar plexus and spleen chakras. She noted that the throat center seemed unusually closely connected with the solar plexus, and that the spleen was abnormal. This caused her to wonder what the blood count was. The colors of the spleen chakra were pale and fewer than normal. (The reader will remember that the colors of this center usually repeat those of all the other centers.) There was a disarrangement in the petals that supply energy to the solar plexus. The spleen center was also slightly out of alignment and for this reason unable to process and distribute the normal supply of energy to the other centers. Because of these abnormalities, DVK looked at the astral spleen chakra as well, and noted that its ruddy color was paler than normal, that its movement was jerky and its form droopy, and that it had a tendency to take in energy and then close up.

All these functional abnormalities, and especially the observation about the blood count, correlated well with the medical diagnosis.

The Sacral Chakra

This center is related to the gonads, a term which includes both male and female reproductive glands.

The ovaries are two glands in the female that produce the reproductive cell, the ovum, and two known hormones. They are almond-shaped bodies lying on either side of the pelvic cavity, and are attached to the uterus by the utero-ovarian ligaments. They are four centimeters in length, two centimeters in width and one-and-a-half centimeters in thickness.

The structure of each ovary consists of two parts, an outer portion called the cortex, which encloses a central medulla. The cortex produces the ova and the hormone estrogen. Progesterone is secreted by a reddish yellow mass of tissue called the corpus luteum. The activity of the ovaries is controlled primarily by the gonadotropic hormones of the pituitary follicle stimulating hormone (FSH) and the luteinizing hormone (LH).

The male gonads or testicles, two reproductive glands, are located in the scrotum and produce the male reproductive cell or spermatozoa and the male hormone testosterone, a steroid. Each testicle is about four centimeters long, two-and-a-half centimeters in width and thickness, and enclosed in a dense inelastic fibrous membrane. The male hormone testosterone stimulates the production of the secondary sexual characteristics and is essential for normal sexual behavior.

DVK has observed that the sacral chakra is the only center in which the direction of movement is different in men and women. The male etheric chakra is a much darker shade of red, and turns in a clockwise direction. In contrast, the female etheric chakra is an orange-red and turns counterclockwise.

Seen clairvoyantly, normal ovaries are characterized by pulsating and sparkling light. If the ovary has cysts, the brightness diminishes; if one ovary is removed, that light vanishes but can still be seen in the remaining ovary. If both ovaries and uterus are removed, changes can be seen in the sacral chakra. The red color which is normal in the core becomes more orange, and the petals more yellow. The size of the center remains the same, however.

Diseases Related to the Sacral Chakra

Medical textbooks describe "hot flashes" as a phenomenon whose mechanism and pathology are obscure. Hot flashes are common in women at menopause when the ovarian hormones are diminished, or when the ovaries are surgically removed. There is usually a subjective sensation of heat, mainly in the chest, neck and face, which in severe cases may extend all over the body. This is immediately accompanied by a flushing of the skin and sweating, which lasts a few minutes. The intervals between the hot flashes vary from subject to subject, and may occur every hour on the hour, or every six to eight hours. If asleep, women are known to throw off their bed covers to cool off. Some women take the female sex hormone estrogen to inhibit the hot flashes; others prefer to let nature take its course.

DVK was asked to observe a patient who had frequent attacks of hot flashes. Subsequently, it was possible to repeat the observation a number of times, and on several occasions she saw the subject before any symptoms were outwardly apparent.

DVK reported that the etheric energy emanating from the pituitary gland was shooting towards the ovaries to stimulate them, as is the normal pattern. But since the subject had had both ovaries excised, no response was forthcoming. The pituitary gland responded by increasing its etheric stream, in an effort to stimulate the ovarian hormones, but to no avail. (It is known that the pituitary gland hormones have an effect on the menstrual cycle.) In consequence, the pituitary gland seemed to send a strong signal to the thyroid gland, calling it into action, as it were, to compensate for the lack of ovarian response. The thyroid, being to some degree in control of body temperature, increased its activity by vasodilatation of the blood vessels and perspiration.

DVK described this interaction as a pulsating light shooting at the different endocrine glands. When the glands responded, a sparkling luminosity was perceived. When there was no response from the target gland, the thyroid glandular system responded to the stimulus of the pituitary.

Another patient was referred to us for a spot evaluation. She had had a tumor of the rectum for two years, and a year later she had developed a tumor of the breast. A right ovarian cyst was diagnosed by a gynecologist.

DVK noted that in the right ovary the flow of etheric energy to the pituitary gland was partially blocked. The ovary appeared to be the size of a tennis ball, and its surface looked more spongy than its core. The left ovary seemed normal. Also the pituitary gland was not functioning as actively on the right side as on the left.

In this case, DVK's observation of the general etheric field and the organs was sufficient for her diagnosis— which correlated well with the medical history—and no detailed analysis of the chakras was made.

The Root Chakra

There are no relationships between the root chakra and any of the major endocrine glands. However, DVK stated that she perceived a very small gland, about the size of a pea, located at the base of the spine. This is the glomus coccygeum, sometimes known as the coccygeal body. It was first described by the anatomist Luschkas (1820-1875), but its function is still not well documented. The coccygeal gland is placed near the tip of the coccyx at the base of the spine, and is about two and a half millimeters in diameter, with an irregular oval shape. Sometimes several smaller nodules are found around or near the main mass. There are also astral and mental counterparts of this tiny gland.

The root chakra is traditionally connected with the kundalini, which is not normally active in the average person. Etherically, this center has some relationship with the brain and the pineal gland, for it is especially interrelated with the crown chakra, with open interconnections in some states of consciousness. However, the root chakra helps energize all the other centers as well.

During the course of her observations of different people, DVK noted varying degrees of brightness in this center. When the energies of the root chakra are vitalized, its color becomes uniformly yellowish-orange, and the three spinal energies, ida, pingala and sushumna, stream from its core in a flow which is both wide and bright. This indicates spiritual development of a high order.

No case histories related to this center were investigated.

XII
Diseases Related to Consciousness and the Brain

In previous chapters, data were presented with respect to clairvoyant observations of changes in the chakras and corresponding areas of the energy fields. In this chapter the focus is upon displacement and malfunctioning of the etheric energy in the brain and the resulting clinical defects.

Since DVK had no knowledge of anatomical terms, we used a Life/Form replica of the brain by Nasco on which she could indicate her observations. This was a bisected human head including the neck, made from an actual dissection of a human brain molded and cast in vinyl rubber. DVK was given a brief demonstration of the anatomical pathways, so that she could note any changes she might perceive in both normal and abnormal states. To give her further tangible knowledge of the brain, she was taken to the neuroanatomy department of a medical school and shown both a total human brain and one that was sliced in sections.

Many of DVK's observations concern the cerebellum, a part of the brain between the brain stem and the back of the cerebum (diagram 1). It is concerned especially with coordination of all the muscles and with the equilibrium of the body. In order to set DVK's observations of the brain and spine in the proper context, we quote the following description from Gray's *Anatomy*:

Anatomically the cerebellum consists of a narrow median portion called the vermis, which is located between two laterally and posteriorly protruding cerebellar hemispheres, located dorsal to pons and medulla oblongata. It appears to serve as a suprasegmental coordinator of muscular activities, especially those of motor functions that require sequential, repetitive or complex movements. It helps regulate muscle tone and maintain proper balance for standing, walking and running.

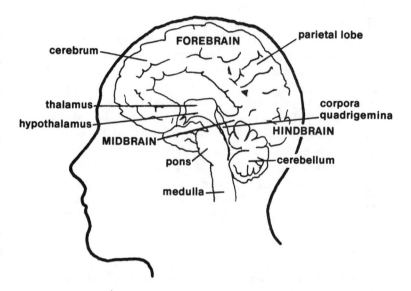

Diagram 1. Cross section of the brain within the skull, showing the approximate location of various structures referred to in the text.

According to DVK, the etheric energy flows from the base of the spine into the medulla oblongata, the part of the brain that joins the spine (see diagram), where there is a small energy vortex. This center, however, seems to be more important on the astral than on the etheric level. The etheric cerebellum seems to be a receptive organ and is therefore able to absorb surplus energy from the rest of the brain. It seems to act as a sort of sponge or shock-absorber for the overflow of etheric energy. In children, the cerebellum is perceived as being more active in the center than on the periphery, whereas in adults the reverse is true. (It is worth noting that tumors of the central portion of the cerebellum, known as the vermis, occur mainly in children.)

There is a direct connection between the cerebellum and the crown chakra at the etheric level.

The thalamus (diagram 1) seems to have a positive etheric charge, which is balanced by the negative or minus charge in the cerebellum. The etheric energy of the brain seems to be released and discharged through the region of the brain connected with the thalamus. This may have an overcharge of energy, to which the cerebellum, with its negative charge, acts as a neutralizer.

A system is formed by the cerebellum and the caudate nucleus (which is part of the floor of the lateral ventricle, one of the cavities continuous with the spinal column). It was DVK's impression that the two caudate nuclei and the two portions of the cerebellum act together, and have a balancing and protective effect. The various sections of the brain are all interrelated with the nervous system via the cerebrospinal fluid, which is the agent responsive to electrical discharges. It seems to act as a conductor of energy in the brain and spine, and may also serve this function with respect to levels of energy higher than the physical.

The crown chakra, as well as the pineal gland, pons and midbrain (diagram 1) probably have more to do with conscious perception than is currently believed.

The flow of energy up the sushumna or etheric channel from the chakra at the base of the spine to the medulla oblongata (diagram 1) may have some effect on the cerebrospinal fluid and its level of energy. In the average person, this flow in the sushumna is rather slow, but it is swift and powerful in a spiritually developed person. If the kundalini energy at the base of the spine has been aroused and flows up the spine to the medulla oblongata, this produces an effect not only on the brain but on the total energy of the body.

Etherically, the alta major center is a small area where the cranium and the spine approximate contact. When fully developed, it forms a center of communication between the vital energy of the spinal column and that of the crown and brow chakras.

Dyslexia

The word "dyslexia" comes from the Greek. The term is used in psychology to identify cases where there is serious difficulty with reading words or numbers. It is a condition in which a person with normal vision is unable to interpret written words correctly because of a disturbance in visual perception. In most cases the subject confuses letters or numbers: b may be seen as d, or p as q, or the letters may also be reversed vertically, as in n and u, or w and m. In the same way, the numbers 6 and 9 or 5 and 8 may be misread. Auditory and tactile stimuli are often normal and therefore play a part in training the patient to overcome the handicap.

DVK was asked to trace the etheric pathways concerned with vision, first in a normal and then in a dyslexic brain, in the hope that the mechanism of the defects could be discovered. With the aid of the Life/Form model of the brain, she could point more precisely to the areas she perceived as deviating from normal.

In general, she observed that in dyslexia there is a slight local dislodgement of the etheric field from the brain material in certain segments of the visual pathways. It seemed to her as though the visual pathways had not made what she called a sufficient "grooving" in the brain substance. It should be noted that dyslexia is a local defect.

In 1973, DVK observed CT, a woman with three children who had been dyslexic since childhood. CT felt a slight "block" when reading the letters b and d and the numbers 5 and 8 or 6 and 3, and she also had difficulty in retaining numbers in her memory. She was unable to use a calculator because of her difficulty in hitting the right numbers. Her son, JT, aged fifteen, showed a greater degree of dyslexia. Many years before we saw them, both mother and son had received training to overcome their visual disability by using the sense of touch.

When DVK was asked to look specifically at the brains of both these subjects, she described the abnormalities as a fluctuating pattern—a slight "time lag"—between the etheric impulses from the corpora quadrigemina in the midbrain to the parietal lobe, the sensory and motor area of the brain (diagram 1). This abnormality was more marked in the son than in the mother, although DVK did not know that he had the more severe case of dyslexia. When CT became anxious, she blocked the flow of etheric energy, and thus slowed down the mechanism which DVK called "interpreting the seeing."

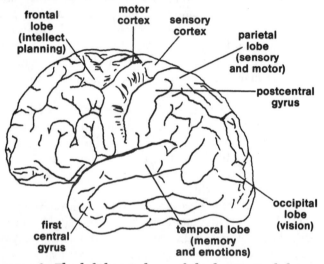

Diagram 2. The left hemisphere of the brain. Each hemisphere is divided into four lobes, the frontal, parietal, occipital, and temporal. The lobes have specialized functions. A gyrus is a convolution of the brain.

When CT was given a page to read, DVK observed a slight slowing down on both sides of the parietal lobes, but when sound was used there was a slight increase in the brightness around the area of the first temporal gyrus, where auditory impressions are received and interpreted in the brain (diagram 2). (This observation was in agreement with the medical data.)[1] Because of this brightness, DVK thought that the use of melodious sound could help her to synchronize the pattern and overcome the difficulty of visual interpretation. Her sensitivity to sound was observed to be more on the left than the right side in the temporal area. Since she was more developed in the auditory portion of the brain than in the visual, music had a definite effect on her emotions.

When single numbers were written on a piece of paper and flashed before CT's eyes, DVK observed that the receptivity in the right parietal region was not as good as on the left, as though the right side had more to do with numbers than letters. CT had a memory lag with respect to visual perception of numbers, related to seeing the number physically and remembering it.

Her general etheric was slightly loose and coarse. When she experienced an emotional reaction to a situation, she tended to feel woozy and tired, and was unable to think clearly. Her emotions dominated her, due to the strong connections between the loose etheric and the astral body, and these strong emotional reactions in turn produced fluctuations in her physical strength.

The astral body appeared volatile, and its movement was both intense and very rapid. There was resentment and insecurity, with a long-established anxiety, and she was unable to let go of this pattern. Music, however, helped to release her from the grip of these emotions and gave her great satisfaction. She had formerly sung publicly, but when it was suggested that a resumption of her singing might help her to relax, she replied, "I need an audience."

Her son, JT, tended to confuse the letters *b* with *d* and *p* with *q* when reading. He had received some training to overcome this handicap.

---

1. Posterior nuclei of the corpora quadragemini are in fact concerned with the auditory reflex.

With the aid of the brain model, DVK pointed out how she perceived the visual impulses in a normal person. In the case of a dyslexic, there was a slight slowing in the etheric brain pattern, and as a result the impulses from the optic nerve to the region of the corpora quadrigemina were slightly delayed as they travelled to the parietal region for visual interpretation (see diagram 1). There was a minimum delay, with dyssynchronicity on the left as compared to the right.

DVK pointed to an area on the Life/Form brain model about two centimeters above the first temporal gyrus. When JT was asked to read, DVK observed his etheric brain pattern and noticed that when he came to the letters *b* and *d*, there were slight hesitations in his reading. These seemed to be related to the parietal region which reacted more slowly, as though the track of the nerve impulses was slower and wider than in the average person. A time lag in the mammillary body in the hypothalamus was also noticed.

When single letters such as *p* and *q* written on a slip of paper were unexpectedly flashed before JT's eyes, DVK observed that there was a split second's delay, as though the visual impulses were slightly deviated to another section of the brain before he could focus on them and get the correct interpretation. However, when the experiment was repeated several times and he became aware of which letters he would see, his reading improved. It was as though the focusing of his attention corrected the side-tracking of the etheric energy. This may explain how and why tactile and visual stimuli used in training the dyslexic child can help make the electrical impulse "groove" along a more consistent pattern, and focus in the right area for interpreting the visual stimuli. When the letters *k* or *g* were presented to JT visually, the process of transmission within the brain seemed normal.

In 1981, Drs. Albert Galaburdo and Thomas Kemper of Boston pointed to noticeable anatomical differences between dyslexic and normal readers' brains. They studied young people who had died in their early twenties and found unusual arrangements of cells, which suggested to them that the language areas were disturbed on either side of the brain. This finding confirms DVK's clairvoyant observations.

Autism

Autism is defined as an inborn brain disturbance, particularly in the sequencing of sounds and experience. A severe language problem is a key symptom. It is a syndrome appearing in childhood, with symptoms of self-absorption, inaccessibility, aloneness, inability to relate to others, with highly repetitive play and at times rage reactions. The autistic child exhibits bizarre muscular movements of both arms and legs, has difficulty speaking and is unable to communicate adequately.

Autistic children have been misunderstood and at times mistreated because of medical ignorance of the mechanism and causative factors of the disorder. Parents, especially mothers, have been held responsible to some degree for the condition of the child, and made to feel guilty. As our knowledge improves, we will reach a more correct understanding of this very serious abnormality. In 1972, after seeing children presented on a television program, SK became convinced that autism is a neurological rather than a psychological disorder.

DVK was taken to visit an autistic child in his home, as well as to a school where she was able to observe autism, Down's syndrome and children with other abnormalities.

In October, 1972, we visited the home of Billy, an autistic child. On our arrival, Billy, who was a handsome boy of fourteen, appeared at the front door and assumed a strange position, with one leg twisted and an arm bent in an angular position. His eyes were alert, cold and glassy. There was no warmth of expression in his face, nor was there any response to our efforts to make contact with him. He stood in that awkward position for a few moments and then suddenly moved swiftly into the house.

All during our visit, Billy would wander restlessly in

and out of the room; unable to sit in one position, he would rock back and forth and then suddenly jump up and walk away. His general body movements were bird-like, and his arm and leg motions were angular rather than smooth. There was no paralysis or weakness in any part of his body, and his gross physical coordination, such as in running, seemed good.

Finer movements of the hands, which require dexterity, seemed difficult for Billy to coordinate, but he was able to sign his name. When rock music was played, he responded to the rhythm and reacted physically in a distorted way. His voice was monotonous and flat. He understood simple questions but could not comprehend or respond to abstract ideas. He often watched television but would turn the sound off. He had good recall for the names of actors in a television program he watched, yet he was unable to say what the program was about. His mother was kind to him but firm, and he always obeyed her.

DVK observed a disturbance in the etheric brain. The electrical brain pattern on the left side around the area of the postcentral gyrus was abnormal (diagram 2). DVK usually observes two major circuits in the brain which she calls "loops": small loops near the surface of the brain (that is, the gray matter), and larger loops which connect the surface of the brain (the gray matter) to the deeper parts (the midbrain and other nuclei). In a normal person the two circuits seem to be synchronized, but DVK observed that in an autistic child there is no synchronization.

In the smaller circuits seen on the surface of the brain, the electrical impulses in the autistic child were slower than normal, duller and less vital. The larger circuits (the interconnections with the other nuclei, the thalamus, midbrain, etc.) were slow and, not being synchronized with the smaller circuits, they appeared to act independently at times. This produced the jerky movements. The right side of the brain was not as disturbed etherically as the left, which did not function adequately when the boy tried to speak. The electrical impulses moving within the brain were slow. He could visualize and think in concrete terms about objects like a cat or chair, but words involving concepts, such as "school," were beyond him.

Etherically, the area at the top of the head had a dull section like a pocket within it. There was a general slowing down and a lack of coordination of the nerve impulses. This may explain the absence of logical deduction and the ability to understand abstract ideas and form a holistic point of view. The lack of synchronization within the inner brain circuitry would also explain the poor coordination, both in speech and in bodily movements. His knees were bent in an angular position, and he walked almost sideways at times.

The form of the crown chakra was abnormal and its periphery was uneven, which influenced the outflow of etheric energy to the physical brain.

There was a striking disalignment between the etheric, astral and mental fields. They did not mesh correctly, and the result was a gap between them. This led not only to a dysrhythmia among the three fields, but also to their dysfunction. For example, if an idea came into Billy's mind and he started to think about it, he could complete a single idea, but there was a gap between the coordination of the mind and physical expression in speech. This resulted in difficulty in synchronizing the idea with its verbal expression. The effect was that he could love his father or his mother at any single time, but he could not think of both of them simultaneously.

The etheric field showed no disease process, only a lack of coordination. The impulses were received slowly, so that there was a time lag in registering impressions from the outside world. To overcome this, it was necessary to repeat things to him slowly and carefully.

The astral body was smaller than normal, underdeveloped and dull, with only few faint and pale colors. Billy did not feel strong emotion, but when he did it affected him adversely. He then tended to stiffen and block off his mental body as well as his physical. For example, if he had an outburst of anger, he would suddenly stiffen and stand still for a moment, and his physical reactions would slow down. This was partly due to the dysfunction and lack of synchronization of the long circuits of the brain. In a normal person there is an almost instantaneous co-ordination between the emotional and the etheric/physical bodies, but in Billy's case he was physically incapable of reacting quickly. Because of this he was not dangerous, even when screaming in anger.

The mental body was also small in size, with little color, showing that his ideas were limited and poorly developed. There was a lack of synchronicity between the mental and astral fields due to their weak connection, dysrhythmia and poor coordination.

The etheric brow chakra showed abnormality and some disturbance in the core and in the circulation of energy near the pituitary, although the gland itself appeared normal enough within certain limits.

DVK's general conclusion was that autism appears to be a condition of malfunction in the nerve impulses between the gray matter of the brain and other centers. The displacement of the etheric from the brain substance is very severe. There is both lack of synchronization and of integration among the etheric, astral and mental levels, and in addition there is a gap in the interconnections at the etheric field.

Down's Syndrome

Down's syndrome is a severe form of mental deficiency or retardation which involves an extra chromosome (number 21). Children afflicted with Down's syndrome characteristically have a small head, slanting eyes with an inner (epicanthic) fold of the upper eyelids (hence often called "Mongoloid") and a fissured tongue that is usually large and protruding. One in eight mentally defective children exhibits Down's syndrome, which may be described as a delimiting disease, slow functioning, that tends to affect or limit the way the electrical impulses are sensed in the brain cortex.

Michael, aged six years, was seen in October 1972. In

his case, the most striking disturbances were found in the etheric regions of the pituitary, thyroid and thymus glands, as well as in the cerebellum. The left side of the etheric brain had a short circuitry mechanism dealing with the whole periphery of the brain. There was a regular slowing down, although parts of the brain received spurts of energy which caused his physical movements. In contrast to the autistic child who becomes locked into certain bodily positions, Michael's movements were compulsive.

The hormonal balance of the pituitary gland was abnormal, so that it did not function properly. DVK stated that the pituitary has an effect on the whole physical body, including the hands and feet. (In acromegaly, a disease of the pituitary gland, the hands, feet and head become greatly enlarged.) Also, this gland affects the release of all the hormones into the body. (This too is medically correct.)

Michael's thyroid was also abnormal in its functioning, both in itself and in conjunction with the pituitary, indicating an imbalance between the two. There was in addition an imbalance between the thyroid and the thymus glands, with more activity in the thymus than in the average person.

The cerebellum seemed to inhibit the energy system, and thus normal mental development did not occur.

The etheric crown chakra was smaller than average, and the core was also small, although within normal limits. The rhythm was slow and the color dull, with irregularities in the petals.

The whole etheric body was within the average range, but looser in texture than is usual.

The astral body displayed fewer colors than normal, but more than in an autistic child. Its predominant color was a reddish-rose, signifying some affection. The texture was expandable, but the emotional reactions were short-lived, and the span of attention brief.

Although the mental body showed some abnormalities, it was of better quality than that of the autistic child. There were no inhibitions, and the interconnections between the mental field and the etheric and astral were also better, even though there was some looseness. Because of this, the mental potential of a Down's syndrome child offers some possibility of development as he attempts to make contact with the outside world and wants to please, whereas in the autistic child communication is very difficult.

Obsessive-Compulsive Neurosis

Obsessive-compulsive neurosis is a rare psychiatric syndrome. The patients are usually intelligent and fully aware of their compulsive behavior but unable to break its pattern. This may take the form of constantly washing their hands for fear of infections, or of certain compulsive thoughts which they are unable to get rid of. These compulsive thoughts and actions make it impossible for the patients to function normally in society.

In 1977 DVK saw RS, who at the age of thirteen had become aware of recurrent thoughts about the holy words of the Old Testament. His behavior became ritualistic, and he was continually haunted by the desire to keep the holy books and other things clean and tidy. He also began to hear voices. At the age of fifteen he became aware of admonitions inside his head, exhorting him to wash his hands and clean the books. He was admitted to a mental hospital where he received intensive psychiatric and medical treatment, including massive doses of vitamins, but there was no real improvement in his symptoms, and he was discharged from the hospital.

In 1977 when RS was seen, he described his obsessive mental processes very clearly and acknowledged that they were unreasonable but beyond his control. He had observed, however, that melodious music seemed to soothe and diminish his compulsive thoughts. There were no auditory hallucinations at the time of his examination.

DVK observed that the general etheric field was normal in size, and no major disturbance could be detected, except for a very slight fluctuation in the energy level. There was, however, an imbalance in the rhythm. The left side of the etheric body was smaller and less active than the right. In addition, the etheric was slightly detached from the physical body, and the texture was somewhat porous. There was an inequality in the electrical circuitry in the brain near the region of the hypothalamus. The energy there fluctuated in brightness and became dim near the optic nerve, as though the flow was spotty. The thyroid gland seemed inactive, and its etheric energy was imbalanced. RS was on medication, and it was impossible to judge whether or not the drugs were partly responsible for the disturbances.

The hearing of voices seemed to originate from disturbances in the solar plexus chakra, not from the throat as is more usual. The etheric solar plexus was dysrhythmic and generally "out of kilter." The patient was easily upset emotionally, and during fits of anxiety his etheric energy was lowered, with physical repercussions.

The general shape of the astral body seemed within the normal range, but there was a striking abnormality both at the top of the aura and also on its periphery, which appeared ragged. A large amount of gray appeared in the aura, streaked with red which indicated annoyance. A rather sickly greenish-yellow, which appeared in blotches, indicated jealousy. There was complete dysrhythmia between the two sides of the aura, with more disturbance on the right.

As mentioned previously, the point at which the etheric and astral energy fields come together is the gateway to the astral world. In RS both the etheric and astral levels of the solar plexus chakra were dysrhythmic in a fashion which DVK called "rocking," and their interrelationship was abnormal.

The mental body was moderately clear, showing that the thought processes were working, but more slowly than normal. RS had the ability to coordinate his thoughts, but not to project them. The mental body was less dysrhythmic than the astral and etheric fields; he was capable of producing a thought, but not of identifying himself with it.

Most importantly, his thinking had no effect on his emotions; it was as though thinking and feeling were in two separate compartments. He could think but could not carry out his thoughts, for the mechanism of implementation requires that thought be transmitted from the mental through the astral to the etheric level. It was between the mental and astral that his block occurred. The negation of thinking was what created RS's compulsion. Since he was self-centered, his etheric energy was cut off as it flowed inward with little outflow, and this diminished the vitality of the etheric body.

This patient suffered the most dysrhythmia involving all three energy fields—etheric, emotional and mental—that DVK had ever seen. The interrelatedness between the astral and the mental was exceptionally poor. For example, at one moment he might be able to think and analyze a problem, but in the next moment his emotions would "wobble" and throw him off balance. The interlocking mechanism between the mental and astral bodies was not properly aligned, and therefore the causal and mental fields were unable to control the emotional.

He was extremely fearful of making a decision. Whenever he thought of something to do, the negative aspect of the idea would arise, so that he would feel as though he did not want to act on it. He was full of fear, accompanied by fits of anxiety.

DVK suggested that it would help him if he were given small tasks to do and was made to carry them to completion. He needed to be forced to break through his inability to make a decision. At the same time, he should be helped to find satisfaction in small achievements.

What emerged most clearly from this case history was the fact that the interrelationships between the various bodies or fields are extremely important, for it is these which create the integration of the personality and make action possible.

Manic-Depressive States

Several cases of manic-depression were seen by us, two of which are fairly typical.

VJ, aged twenty-five, married with two children, was diagnosed in 1979 as manic-depressive with schizophrenic features. At the age of sixteen she had attempted suicide and showed abnormal behavior patterns; she was not hospitalized but was treated at home. In February, 1979, she made another suicide attempt; in June of the same year, after setting fire to her home, she was admitted to a mental hospital. In a few months she made a temporary recovery, but in 1980 she succeeded in committing suicide by taking an overdose of drugs.

She was seen by DVK in June and November of 1979. She had been suffering from recurring episodes of hearing voices and seeing visions. There was a loss of appetite and disturbance in her sleep rhythm.

DVK observed that the patient had had a rapid flow of etheric energy all her life, with constantly changing patterns. The core of the etheric solar plexus chakra was dysrhythmic and out of harmony with its astral counterpart, which was her primary source of trouble. The patient had a sense of power derived from her active solar plexus, but was unable to handle its energies. She had a "terrible temper" and excessive astral energy which became explosive in different ways. Later, she could not remember what she had done.

When the subject began to sing, DVK observed that the sustained breathing affected the solar plexus. However, she seemed to lose interest quickly, and become frustrated; this in turn opened up the solar plexus center, which became simultaneously more charged with power and more dysrhythmic. In short, the astral and etheric levels of the solar plexus chakra could not handle the energies she generated.

The etheric brow center showed the same type of dysrhythmia as the solar plexus, with some looseness in the periphery of the center. The etheric crown chakra exhibited dysrhythmia in the petals and looseness in the periphery of the center.

DVK tried to help the patient stabilize the solar plexus center by showing her a deep-breathing technique, which might help relax her and repair the breaks in the solar plexus chakra. The patient had a strong desire to heal others but not to love them, and she was filled with resentment toward life. Unfortunately, she committed suicide the following year.

Another case of manic-depression was that of VT, a student at Harvard University whose main complaint was an inability to apply himself to his work. This condition had persisted for three years.

The patient's family history revealed mental illness on the maternal side, with manic-depressive symptoms. A maternal great-uncle had committed suicide. On the paternal side there was evidence of mood swings and a tendency toward delusions of grandeur. The father was a writer who was moody, apprehensive and unable to control his emotions.

DVK saw him in 1955, when the subject was depressed and suicidal. He was oversensitive and disturbed by noises around him. His general etheric was observed to be misty blue, with a variable mixture of color. The luminosity was above average, and the movement was rhythmic and also above average. The size was normal, but the energy field was wider on the left side of the body and droopy in the solar plexus area. Elasticity was average and the texture fine, but there were slight breaks all over the etheric body, indicating a tendency to psychosomatic disturbances.

Schizophrenia

PCK was a patient in a mental hospital, having been diagnosed as suffering from paranoid schizophrenia. He was brought to us for evaluation in 1960.

When DVK observed him, she noted that the etheric crown chakra was grayer in the petals than in the core, indicating a definite malfunction. The degree of luminosity was low, the movement dysrhythmic as well as variable, both in the core and in the petals. The form also deviated from the norm, as the periphery of the petals were toothed like a saw. The edges of the core itself were irregular, but even more unusual was a split going through the whole chakra from front to back at the six o'clock/twelve o'clock axis, producing a severe dysrhythmia.

There was a slight leakage of energy resulting from the lack of sharp definition in the core of the chakra. The texture of the whole center was both coarse and loose, and its elasticity was poor. The grayness produced abnormality; gray "clouds" in the core of the chakra tended to block him off from the higher levels of the self. Because of this, his emotions tended to take over, and he had no self-control.

The thalamus was marked with irregular impulses of etheric energy which had the effect of delaying the rhythm, and the pineal gland was not functioning normally.

The etheric brow chakra was also tinged with gray in both of its components, which indicated a malfunctioning. Some red as well as gray was seen in the core, and gray, red and green in the petals. The size was within the normal range, but the luminosity was dull and the speed of movement was both variable and dysrhythmic. The shape deviated from the norm, in that the periphery was ragged, and there was a peculiar "banding" of the whole chakra, some normal bands being interposed between those that were abnormal. The core was split in the center like the crown chakra, with a ragged periphery. The elasticity was poor, and the texture of both core and petals was both coarse and loose. The function of this chakra was abnormal, as indicated by the gray color and the irregular movement affected perception and visualization. The pituitary gland was within the normal range.

In the etheric throat chakra, the petals were blue and gray, with a very dark blue, almost black, core. This indicated that PCK was blocking out his higher self. The luminosity was dull, and the movement of both core and petals was dysrhythmic, with a speed which varied from slow to average. The size was within normal, but the petals were slightly droopy, with a leakage of energy at a point near the six o'clock area. The elasticity was poor, the texture coarse and loose, and the function of the thyroid was variable.

The etheric solar plexus chakra was dull and abnormal, and the petals were yellow, gray and red. Here, the red indicated anger which took over, and controlled his behavior. At such moments there was a transfer of the primary seat of consciousness from the crown chakra to the solar plexus.

DVK summed up by noting that the most striking feature in this case was the split in all of the chakras. In addition, the relationship between the etheric and the astral, where the predominance of gray indicated depression, was unusual.

The checklist made at the time of the interview, upon which the foregoing account is based, will be found in the section of the appendix on consciousness and the brain.

A final note: Our assignment of cases to a particular chakra or aspect of the etheric may sometimes appear arbitrary to the reader. This is especially true of the cases related to the crown chakra and those linked to consciousness and the brain. A good deal of overlap may be perceived. The reader will note that we have assigned cases of epilepsy to the section on the crown chakra in Chapter XI (although the brain is obviously involved as well); this is because etheric changes in the crown chakra are highly conspicuous in this disease. However, we must reemphasize that there is no separation between the chakra system and the etheric counterparts of brain and organs; all work together as one whole. The classifications we have made were principally for the purposes of clarity.

XIII
Effects of Drugs and Other Modifiers of the Fields

From the description of the etheric given in Chapter IV, it should be clear that this field is material in a sense which is quite different from either the astral or mental, since it is inseparable from the physical body and perishes with it at death.

Clairvoyants have repeatedly stated that in their experience physical factors or materials do not modify the etheric field. Yet they also report that liquids and gases as well as solids have etheric counterparts. In fact, the etheric field is said to be subdivided into several categories, the densest of which is associated with physical solids, while the more rarefied are nonphysical. Some observers have even postulated that the electron is an aspect of the etheric.

If any of the above is true, there must be physical factors that could modify the etheric field. One of our early experiments has bearing on this question. DVK was taken to the Presbyterian Medical Center in New York City to observe both normal and radioactive iodine solutions. Both of these are as crystal clear as water, and DVK was not told which tube contained the radioactive solution. However, when she observed them clairvoyantly she immediately picked out the radioactive tube as having more etheric luminosity than the normal iodine solution.

The technician was then asked to place the radioactive iodine test tube in the lead well, which is a container that inhibits the radioactivity's escape into the atmosphere. After a few minutes, DVK reported that the luminosity inside the lead well had increased. At first this effect seemed inconsistent, since the lead casing was supposed to be inhibiting the escape of the radioactivity. Therefore, how could DVK say it had increased? On second thought, however, this observation made a great deal of sense. To DVK's etheric vision, the lead container was no impediment whatsoever; she saw right through it. Since the radioactive iodine constrained by the lead well could not escape as it would under normal conditions, its etheric luminosity was enhanced.

Attempts were made to use other experimental methods in order to discover what materials or solutions, if any, could modify the etheric field. The following examples may at first sight appear very simple, but they help us to understand both the potential and the limits of etheric vision.

Two cups of water, one cold and one warm, were placed two feet away from DVK in a dark room, and she was asked to describe them etherically. She said that one of the cups showed a slight increase of etheric energy on its surface, and she therefore assumed that it was the one containing warm water. This was correct.

DVK observed that manmade materials, such as nylon and dacron, partially inhibit the freedom of the etheric flow, which may be why some people find them uncomfortable to wear. She perceived the reverse to be true with respect to cotton, wool and silk.

Sound, Light and Magnetism

Some people are sensitive to very high or very low sound frequencies. Similarly, certain sounds can make us edgy and restless, while others soothe and harmonize. The beat of rock music affects people in different parts of the body, and may be physically or sexually stimulating.

Some report feeling musical vibrations throughout their bodies; others feel them in the arms or legs, back or head. It is well known medically that a person who listens to very loud music over a period of time may damage the hearing for certain frequencies, resulting in partial tone deafness. Classical or religious music, on the other hand, may stimulate the heart and/or the crown chakra.

Certain sound frequencies are being used today both in medical diagnosis and therapeutic procedures. We can cut with ultrasound, shatter a kidney stone, liquify a cataract, photograph the maturing of an ovum or the deposits of calcium in an artery. Undoubtedly, when it is properly understood, sound will be used in the healing and repairing of tissues. But for these advances we need to know more about the effect of sound on biological systems.

Sunlight in small amounts is very beneficial and increases the etheric vitality, but a prolonged exposure to the sun tends to deplete one. Colored lights have varying effects. Yellow and gold light energizes; blue is soothing in cases of infection, reduces pain and lowers blood pressure; green has a harmonizing effect on the etheric. DVK observed that when yellow light was shone on a dog in shock it had a vitalizing effect on the animal's etheric field.

In this connection, it should be noted that there is some difference in the effects produced by the physical use of colored light and the mental visualization of the same color, although the visualization of blue light is effective in pain relief. The form in which the color is used or visualized—such as a circle, a cross or a triangle—may also produce different effects. More research is needed to clarify this area of study. Fluorescent lights produce unpleasant sensations in some sensitives. For example, one healer, FF, could not stand fluorescent light on her hands.

Over 130 years ago, Reichenbach reported the effects which magnetic fields had on some sensitives. He found that those who could feel the presence of a magnet of certain strength, when it was moved up and down the spine without touching the skin, were also sensitive to weather changes and magnetic storms. A few of these sensitives could sleep comfortably only in a north/south position. Unfortunately, we were unable to test DVK's perception of the influence of magnetic fields on any patients.

Geological Factors

A few subjects have reported suffering a depletion of vitality when visiting certain places, either in a city or in the country. They usually have an urge to leave the spot quickly, and after doing so feel revitalized. Two persons known to be sensitive felt very peculiar when visiting so-called magnetic spots; they were slightly nauseated and unable to drive a car for several hours. EP was a sensitive who used her body's responses in dowsing, not only for water but also for minerals and archaeological finds. Another man, a petroleum geologist, reported that he knew where oil was to be found because he felt certain specific sensations in his feet when standing on the ground above it.

Human energy exchange should also be mentioned. It has already been explained that some people with whom we come into close contact can modify our energy fields, either by enhancing or sapping our vitality. This holds true also on the astral and mental levels, for some people are able to uplift our emotions and stimulate our minds, while others deaden and deplete us. This ability will be discussed further in the chapter on healing.

Painkillers

DVK was asked to observe throughout a day the changes in a subject before and after taking Bufferin to alleviate pain. The patient had twisted his right hip while entering a taxi in heavy traffic, and the pain which developed had persisted for several months. While sitting or walking, he felt tightness and pain stretching from the right sacrum or vertebrae in the pelvis to the back of the right thigh and calf of the right leg, but no pain while lying flat.

DVK noted that a sense of pressure had developed along the sacroilliac nerves, which were somewhat irritated, and this produced a swelling. This resulted in pressure on the nerves, which gave rise to the pain when the subject walked or bent over. DVK reported that all the joints were normal, an observation later verified by X-rays. In her opinion, the main problem was in the tendons and muscles, which had been overstretched like an elastic band. There were spurts of broken energy flow, indicating a mild local irritation. The etheric circulation appeared to be reduced around the middle of the thigh, and even more so in the middle of the calf. There was an interruption every few minutes in the flow of etheric energy from the hip to the ankle posteriorly, and thus there was too little energy to nourish the muscles.

Fifteen minutes after the subject took two Bufferin tablets, DVK noted a change in the etheric energy pattern in the region of the brain slightly above the pituitary gland, and this affected the electrical pattern. There was also an increase in the brightness of the energy. The Bufferin seemed to have altered the rhythm of the incoming and outgoing stimuli. A change in the circuitry altered the stimuli coming from different areas of the body. As the energy flowed down the right limb, the impulses seemed to slow down and some dullness was observed. The condition was not cured, but the irritated areas appeared more relaxed. The brain seemed very active, but the Bufferin slowed down the energy to a very small degree in part of the etheric brain, which helped to relax the muscles. The blood flow became more normal, and the rhythm regular.

In half an hour there was further improvement. By then the etheric energy was flowing freely, smoothly and without impediment. The two points that had been observed to be slightly irritated were much better.

After six hours, there was a change in the pattern of etheric energy in the brain. Uneven and jerky impulses were being sent from the sacroilliac region to the brain. In return, the etheric brain tended to send more energy back to the area of pain.

DVK's observations of the effect of Bufferin on the painful muscles was correct in the sense that the patient experienced relief of pain that coincided with changes in the pattern of etheric energy. The pain did return after six hours. In all probability, the area near the pituitary gland DVK referred to is the hypothalamic, and it was here that changes helped increase the flow of blood to the muscles which were lacking etheric energy, relaxing them and thus relieving the pain.

Thorazine

Thorazine (chlorpromazine hydrochloride) is a substance which acts as a depressant of the central nervous system and is employed as a sedative and antiemetic. It also quiets severely excited psychotic patients.

VJ, a married woman of twenty-five with two children, was seen by us in 1979, following an attempted suicide. She was diagnosed as manic-depressive with visual and auditory hallucinations. (See Chapter XII for a fuller discussion of this case history.) After a subsequent suicidal attempt, in which she tried to burn down her home and family, she was observed a second time. VJ was admitted to a mental hospital for several months and then discharged with the recommendation that she take 400 milligrams of Thorazine daily. This seemed to decrease her hallucinations.

Our question was: How does Thorazine act, and what is its mechanism in inhibiting the hallucinations of the mentally ill?

The patient was observed for some time before she took the medication. DVK noted that all the colors of the astral body were disturbed and that her solar plexus was loose and open, causing her to interact excessively with other people. The chakra was unstable, moving too fast, dysrhythmic and abnormally reddish in color. The astral field showed that the rejection system was damaged. The astral body was unstable, and the movement was from left to right, indicating pent-up anger. The colors were dark and muddied and constantly changing. At 4:00 P.M. the patient took 400 milligrams of Thorazine and was observed twenty minutes later by DVK. Since Thorazine is a chemical compound, it has its own etheric counterpart, as does everything in nature. The etheric Thorazine seemed to affect the brain as well as slowing down the brow and throat chakras. This in turn seemed to affect the optic nerve, the hypothalamic region and the pituitary gland, dulling the mechanism of auditory and visual perception. As this was taking place, the patient began to show improvement, although she was still shaken by the memory of her attempt to set her house on fire and her subsequent stay in the mental hospital.

After half an hour, the Thorazine affected all her vehicles, and especially the astral body. The throat and brow chakras were grayer, indicating a slowdown in their activity. Likewise, the pineal gland and the region of the hypothalamus decreased their activity and function, as indicated by a gray color in these areas. The solar plexus chakra was also affected.

In summary, Thorazine's action seemed to decrease the brightness of the etheric body and to depress and close the astral as well as the mental vehicles. This may explain how Thorazine helps the mentally disturbed by blocking and fogging their etheric and astral fields, thus decreasing visual and auditory hallucinations. As DVK's observations continued, the effect of Thorazine was seen to spread to all three vehicles—mental as well as astral and etheric.

Drug Addiction

Probably the most acute social problem facing us today is the widespread use of narcotics and other addictive drugs. Although the data we have to offer are tenuous, scanty and incomplete because of the difficult circumstances

under which we had to work, we offer it in the hope that
it may stimulate others to engage in further research in
this critical field. We were unfortunately not able to get
access to a subject in an acute state of drug intoxication,
nor were we able to observe the withdrawal syndrome.

In May, 1970, we made several visits to an outpatient
clinic which convicted criminal addicts on parole were
required by law to attend. During these visits, we moni-
tored their pupilary reactions, signs of needle pricks and
urinary tests. We were able to sit among the addicts, and
DVK randomly selected the ones to be observed.

The first case was that of a thirty-year-old white man.
The most striking features DVK observed were the etheric
solar plexus, throat and brow chakras. The solar plexus
center was the most disturbed, as indicated by the presence
of a considerable amount of gray and red in both the core
and petals. There was an erratic flow of energy around
the core, with some breaks in the flow pattern as the
energy moved in and out of the chakra. In addition, there
was leakage of the etheric energy. The elasticity was
slack, and the petals were both loose and coarse.

In the throat chakra, the core was tight and dysrhythmic
but its periphery was loose and lax, while the petals'
periphery was both loose and coarse.

The etheric brow chakra indicated that the pituitary
gland was functioning abnormally. It was ejecting a current of energy in a way not usually observed, and it seemed
more active than the rest of the etheric. This raised the
question of whether the state of drug euphoria would be
accompanied with hallucinations or "seeing things."
Whatever he perceived as visual sensations would be
distorted, but not necessarily seen as pictures.

The etheric crown chakra was small and slow.

Because of the patient's stress, he had used up a great
deal of etheric energy, so that at the time the observations
were made both the liver and the adrenals appeared to
be underfunctioning.

The astral body showed a great deal of emotional disturbance and tension, with a tendency to do whatever

occurred to him so long as it didn't involve much effort. There was a low degree of mentality.

In the case of the second patient, a man of forty, the etheric solar plexus chakra was very disturbed, and the vortex was redder in color and faster moving than with the first patient. The center was dysrhythmic, and there was unevenness in the etheric flow. On the other hand, the adrenals were more active than in the first case, and even in a state of agitation. Because of this, DVK assumed that the addiction of this patient was of more recent origin than in the first case.

The core of the etheric throat chakra was tighter than in the first subject, but the petals were looser. Here again, the etheric crown chakra was small and slow. This patient was more dangerous because he had very little self-identity and could therefore be easily influenced. He was very restless, emotionally disturbed and without much self-control.

The third patient was a black man aged thirty. In his case, the etheric solar plexus chakra was more elastic and the petals were loose, dysrhythmic and leaking etheric energy intermittently. The patient showed a tendency to swings between extreme depression and euphoria, fluctuations which were indicated by changes in the solar plexus. The core of the etheric throat chakra was dysrhythmic and loose on its periphery. This affected the levels of energy in both the adrenals and the pituitary gland. The adrenals indicated that the patient had been under great stress for some time, and consequently they were not as active as normal. The etheric crown chakra was also very small and slow. The functioning of the pituitary gland was abnormal, which led to distortion in his perceptions.

The fourth patient was a young Mexican man. Here the etheric solar plexus chakra was dysrhythmic both in the core and in the petals, but to a lesser degree than in the previous patients. The color, however, was a very unpleasant red, with flashes of the same color in the petals. The adrenals were partially overstimulated, and the thyroid indicated some disturbance. The etheric brow chakra seemed faster than normal, but it was beginning to slow down. He did not seem as excited or disturbed as some of the other patients. We did not know, however, the duration of his addiction, nor the length of time he had been free from drug-taking.

In drug addiction, it is as important to treat the imbalance in the astral body, i.e. in the emotions, as it is to treat the etheric. Addicts who were healed at Katherine Kuhlman's meetings received a tremendous astral impact and this helped to change the direction of their emotions. At the same time, healing was taking place at the etheric level, and the simultaneous application of etheric and astral energies seemed to speed up the mechanism of restoration to health. This mechanism was missing in the addicts observed at the outpatient clinic.

In summary, the most outstanding finding in these cases of drug addiction was the dysrhythmia in both the core and the petals of the etheric solar plexus chakra, which affected the whole etheric body. The shade of red, seen in the form of flashes of gray and red or orange and red, differed from that seen in cancer patients, as described in the appendix, where the red was more scarlet. Furthermore, there was a definite decrease in the brightness of the etheric solar plexus chakra, and the leakage there made the patients feel permanently tired. In every case, the adrenal function was lowered.

At the astral level, the solar plexus chakra was greatly disturbed in addicts, with an erratic emotional pattern and periodic lack of energy. In addition, there was disturbance in the relationships between the thyroid, the adrenals, the pituitary gland and the hypothalamic region. The latter tended to produce a type of hallucination, and a loss of the sense of proportion. This dysrhythmia may be temporary, and it might disappear if the patient becomes free of the addiction.

Although these data need further verification, it appears that the effects of narcotics such as morphine and heroin begin at the etheric level and then reach the physical. Obviously opiates are medically useful and necessary, but even with limited use the bridge between the nervous system and the nadis or etheric channels is weakened. Continued use of opiates affects the chakras, and that is when addiction begins. The direction of movement within the chakras is reversed by the drug, and it is this that causes the addiction. In turn, this physiological change in the chakras produces a condition of fear and anxiety in the patient.

XIV
Effects of Surgical Excision

Now that procedures for organ replacement have become so widespread in treating malfunctions of the heart, kidneys and even lungs and liver, the observations we made on the effects of surgery on the etheric field and chakras should have particular interest. Patients who undergo such surgery are forced to take medication to prevent the rejection of the transplanted organ by the body, which regards it as a foreign element and attempts to destroy it. Our research may offer a clue to one of the many factors that determine the rejection syndrome.

In one case of a transplanted kidney, it was observed that the etheric texture of the new kidney did not match the recipient's etheric field in quality; the two did not mesh. The question arises: Is the acceptance or rejection of transplanted organs to some degree dependent on the quality of the etheric of the patient and of the transplanted organ? Could a clairvoyant such as DVK perceive in advance whether rejection would take place and why, and how the rejection mechanism works? This is an interesting problem for research.

In 1984, DVK was taken to observe the patient MB, aged twenty-seven, who had received a kidney transplant in December, 1978, and was hospitalized for a checkup. The main objective was to observe the etheric characteristics and quality of the transplanted kidney as compared with the general etheric field of the patient.

DVK described the etheric of the transplanted kidney as being coarser in texture than the rest of the recipient's etheric body. She remarked, "It is strange to see different qualities of etheric substance in the same person. There is something very odd about the energy in the kidney, as it seems to fluctuate."

The color was darker than the rest of the patient's etheric; the two did not mesh well, and therefore the kidney was not functioning perfectly. DVK also perceived it as being in the front of the abdomen rather than in the back, as is normal. (This observation was correct.) The general etheric was thin and appeared fragmented in the region around the kidney, and the patient had a very low level of energy.

Another of DVK's observations is pertinent here. She discovered that even after a diseased gland was surgically removed, the chakra related to that gland remained visibly abnormal. This fact may offer a clue to the reason why the disease for which the gland was removed may recur. It seems that only when the pattern of the etheric chakra returns to normalcy can the reappearance of symptoms be fully controlled.

DVK also observed that physical disease may arise in a dimension other than the etheric, such as the astral or mental. As previously suggested, psychosomatic medicine may in time come to embrace these dimensions, and thus consider the harmonics between the centers and their respective energy fields. And, to repeat another observation, we do not yet know the factors that determine which physical organ will be the target for disease associated with an abnormal chakra. (See Chapter XI.)

The term "holistic medicine" is used in various ways today, but it usually refers to the concept of the whole person, including body, mind and emotions—and sometimes the self or spirit. Basically, its practitioners emphasize a number of physical modalities other than drugs, such as homeopathy, acupuncture and physical therapy, as well as visualization and other mental techniques. All these techniques are founded upon the concept that disease is an interference with the basic wholeness of the human being, and that healing is accomplished by the restoration of that wholeness. Disease is thus a state of dissonance within the three fields of the personality, and does not describe the condition of the essential self or soul, which is unchanged by disalignments of body, emotions and mind.

Thus holistic medicine should, in its real sense, refer to the elimination of the causes of dissonance in order to promote the healing process and restore normal functioning. In other words, the purpose of medical intervention is to remove the impediments to self-healing.

Phantom Limbs

The rapid advance of techniques for organ replacement raises questions directly related to the effect upon the etheric field of the removal of parts of the physical body. We addressed this problem by having DVK observe a case of what is known as "phantom limbs," a common occurrence in those who have had part of a leg or arm amputated.

Are phantom limbs indeed a phantom, or is there some evidence that they are "real"? The patient feels that the amputated limb is still present, and this often causes severe pain, spasms, itching, a burning sensation and abnormal or bizarre positioning. Over a period of time, the phantom limb seems to move upward toward the stump; this phenomenon is called "telescoping."

Dr. Wilder Penfield of the Montreal Neurological Institute found, in mapping the cerebral cortex of conscious patients during surgery, that the hands and feet have a greater area of representation in the brain than the trunk of the body. Human beings are primarily aware of the fingers and toes, not of the arms and legs. This may have some bearing on the fact that pain in the phantom limb is not illusory; it is a major problem in war casualties and accidents, especially among the young and healthy, for its effects may last a lifetime.

There were several objectives of our investigation. One was to observe a phantom limb etherically, and try to discover why pain, spasms and itching in the phantom limb can be relieved by scratching the healthy normal limb. In the case of chronically ill patients suffering from vascular diseases or diabetes, phantom limbs occur less frequently after amputation and are of shorter duration. What determines the difference between the healthy and the chronically ill patient in such cases? DVK was also asked to note the etheric characteristics of phantom limbs, and how or why massaging the normal limb relieved the pain of the phantom.

GF, a young soldier, stepped on a mine in Vietnam in 1968. The sole of the left foot was damaged, and the foot was amputated just above the ankle in April, 1968. The stump was good, and the heel pad was brought around to make its cushion. The patient was able to use his left foot adequately, but because of phantom pains he was readmitted to the hospital, where the neuromas (masses of nerve tissues in an amputation stump) were removed in the hope of relieving the phantom pains.

We saw the patient in 1970, two months after the last surgery, when the following dialogue took place:

SK: Could you describe the sensation in your amputated foot?

GF: It is a cold feeling—a cold, numb cramp. It feels as if the little toe is sitting on top of the one next to it, and I get pains like a cramp in the arch of my foot.

SK: Do you feel that your left foot is still there?

GF: My toes are definitely there, and so is the arch of my foot, but I cannot feel the rest of it.

SK: How did you learn to relieve the itch in the phantom foot?

GF: I don't know. But if the toes of the amputated foot go into cramp and I can't work it out, I go to the good right foot and rub the toes that are bothering me on the phantom left foot. This seems to help the itch or the cramp. When they told me to do this I thought they were crazy, but it does seem to work.

SK: Has the excision of the neuromas relieved your symptoms?

GF: After the removal of three neuromas at the end of each nerve, the phantom pains remained, but the operation changed the pain in the end of my stump. It has brought the phantom foot closer to the stump; instead of feeling like size 10 it feels like size 6. My toes feel as though they were in the middle of my foot. About a year after the amputation, I felt the toes about an inch from the stump, and as the neuromas grew in, the foot extended again. Immediately after the amputation, the phantom foot was normal in size. When the pain started coming into the stump, my leg was so bad I couldn't walk on it, but now my toes have started going back out and I feel them about halfway through the foot.

SK: Can you move the phantom toes mentally?

GF: I can move the toes on the end of my stump; my toe is right there. (The patient pointed to a place on the stump, and it was observed that he could mentally contract the muscles, which made him feel as though he were moving the phantom limb.)

SK: When you contract the muscles of your stump, does it make you feel that you are actually moving the toe itself?

GF: Well, the big toe is here. (The patient pointed to an area in space about five inches from the stump.)

SK: If I put my fingers near the phantom toes, do you feel that they are being touched?

GF: No.

SK: Can you move the phantom big toe?

GF: Yes.

SK: Can you move the phantom little toe?

GF: No, I can't move it alone, but I can move the whole foot upwards and downwards.

SK: Do you have cramps in the phantom foot?

GF: Yes. If I am up all day with the cast on, then when I am relaxed the toes go into cramps. I have more pain at

night than during the day. I can relieve the cramp or
itching, but I can't separate the little toe from the one
next to it. But I have found one of the quickest ways to
get rid of a cramp is to jump out of bed and put my phantom
foot on the floor. Sometimes I get a sprained phantom ankle!

SK: How do you straighten a twisted phantom ankle?

GF: I don't. I just take off the artificial leg and suffer
for two days.

DVK's observations of GF's phantom left foot were as
follows:

DVK: It seems that the etheric outline of the left foot
is actually there. I do not understand about the telescoping
—there wasn't much removed. It was very close to where
the actual foot was. The etheric energy from the stump
still produces the outline of the toes and the foot, and
indeed there is without a doubt still an etheric foot. He
says he always feels that the foot is there, and I think this
is correct. When he says it feels as if one toe is folded
over another, I do not think this is actually the case, but
there appears to be a "kink" in the etheric energy which
makes the etheric left foot unbalanced. The energy seems
to shoot around the phantom foot irregularly, and therefore there is a corresponding irregularity in the energy
flow up and down the real leg. Since this leg is flesh and
blood, there is a definite energy exchange with the brain,
and when he swings his leg there is a connection in the
spine here. (DVK then pointed to the lumbar region.) I
think this is where part of the difficulty lies.

The connection of a nerve impulse comes from both the
leg and the spine. The impulse to swing his leg, as well as
the pain he feels in the phantom foot come from the
spine. There is in this patient a strong pattern of attachment to the thought of his left foot; in one sense, he hasn't
given it up, because he hasn't acknowledged to himself,
"I am a man without a foot."

I wonder if there shouldn't be some training for amputees
in order to help them accept the loss of a limb. This patient
only had part of his physical foot amputated, so etherically
there was a heel and an outline of his foot not far from

his stump. The outline of the phantom five toes is very clear—much clearer than the heel.

The patient is absolutely certain that he feels the outline of his foot, but he has great deal of pain because of spasm and the feeling that one toe is crossed over another. Etherically, I did not see these toes as crossed, but what I did see was an imbalance of etheric energy between the toes, which produced a similar imbalance on the side of the leg. This may have various physical causes. The patient says he feels more pain when he is relaxed, a condition I do not understand completely. Of course, the fact that he is continually thinking about his nonexistent foot sets up a reaction in his brain, and this reactivates the motion of the spinal energy. There is a reflex action between the nerves, the spine and the mental image of pain. This may be a fact which is not fully recognized.

SK: Did you see etherically how far the phantom toes extended from the stump? Was it five inches from the heel, or more, or less?

DVK: They seem to me at almost the normal position, not where he feels them to be. The foot may be a little smaller and tighter.

SK: What made you think of the spine as an important intermediary between the phantom foot and the brain pattern?

DVK: First of all, there is in reality no toe. But there is a definite etheric connection between the spine and that phantom toe. I thought that this was very abnormal.

SK: Etherically?

DVK: Yes. I was trying to figure out how the man felt the pain. I started with a preconceived idea that the reaction was all in the brain, and then I realized I was absolutely wrong, for the area of pain is very closely connected with the spine. There is certainly a relationship between the brain pattern and the spine, but in this case, the spine is primary.

In summary, GF's amputated toes were brighter than his heel, showed more energy, and were more important to the patient. The minor chakra in the sole of the foot was still visible, although scarcely larger than a pinhead, and this made for trouble. Normally there is no difference between the heel and the toes as respects etheric energy, except that there is more flow in the toes.

o o o o o

A somewhat different case was that of EP, aged 64, who was suffering from diabetes mellitus. Gangrene developed in his right leg due to poor circulation, and it was amputated in August 1969.

The patient developed pain in the phantom limb soon after its amputation. He would feel a desire to scratch his little toe and the bottom of his foot, and at times there would be a pain which felt as though the toes were being twisted and that needles were being stuck into the heel. The sensation of itching was confined to the bottom of the right foot and the lateral side of the right leg. He discovered that scratching the normal left leg relieved the pain and itching in the phantom right foot. He also found that when the itching occurred during the night, if he turned on the light he would convince himself that the leg was not there. This seemed to stop the itch better than anything else. As time went on, he stopped worrying about his phantom limb and found that it became better.

He was first seen by us on May 13, 1970, by which time the phantom limb had almost disappeared. He was no longer aware of it. There were no muscular twitchings or contractions, nor did the amputated foot or leg bother him any longer.

DVK observed that the phantom leg, and even the toes, still showed as a faint outline in the etheric. It looked as though less and less energy was flowing through it. When compared with the case of GP, DVK noticed particularly that there was no thought-form attached to EP's phantom limb, and he seemed to have no basic attachment to the idea of having a leg. The brain was only slightly affected, and that was why there was not much sensation. The etheric energy of the normal leg was quite clear, with a very slight impairment.

Because of his diabetes, we also observed the pancreas and the solar plexus. The chakra was much duller than average, with no red color and a lot of gray. The etheric pancreas also displayed considerable grayness, which indicated a severe case of diabetes. The adrenals were also affected and showed the grayness indicating a disease process.

DVK commented on the fact that, because his leg was gangrenous, a condition which develops slowly and therefore is not as traumatic as a sudden injury to a person in a healthy state, EP might have become used to the idea of having his leg removed. This could have lessened the strength of his thought-form about his lost leg. He seemed to have transferred all his ideas and feelings about it to the normal remaining leg. It seems that the strong attachment to the idea of having a limb is an important factor in the study of phantom limbs.

Anaesthesia and Surgery

The late Dr. Bert Cotton, a heart surgeon, gave us permission to observe his postoperative patients, who were at different stages of recovery from general anaesthesia.

In those who were completely unconscious, DVK observed that the etheric field was squeezed or pushed up so that it hovered around the region of the head, but was not completely exuded from the physical body. In those whose recovery was partial, the etheric field had begun to move downward toward the trunk of the body, and in those who were more awake, the etheric was gradually returning to their feet. It is worth noting that medically and clinically the feet are the last to regain their total sensation after anaesthesia.

Because of the difficulty in obtaining permission to observe postoperative patients, it was decided that we would have easier access to a veterinary hospital for our research. Dr. David Weule was most cooperative in allowing us to use his hospital facilities.

We should mention first that animals have chakra

systems corresponding to those in humans, although the chakras themselves differ in size, color and other characteristics. In dogs the centers are about two centimeters in size, and the brightest etherically is the sacral. Physically, the cerebellum shows little activity and the thymus is small, fairly bright and full of blood.

DVK was asked to describe an animal's etheric field and to identify where she saw abnormalities that indicated disease. Her observations were then compared with Dr. Weule's diagnosis. On a few occasions, she pointed to abnormalities in the animals that Dr. Weule had not yet considered, and these were confirmed a few days or weeks later.

We were trying to understand the characteristics of the etheric field under both local and general anaesthetic, how pain is inhibited and numbness produced, what happens to the etheric field when a tumor or an organ is removed (as in spaying), how healing takes place, and what the effects of drugs are on the etheric body.

In a procedure using local anaesthesia (when one percent Lidocaine Hydrochloride was injected intracutaneously) DVK observed that the flow of etheric energy was diminished locally, and there was increased dullness in the etheric brain.

A cat with a swollen face was being treated with a medication, DMSO (Dimethylsulfoxide). DVK noted that the chemical compound penetrated the basic structure of the skin and cleared the etheric channels very quickly. This may explain the effectiveness of the drug in diminishing swelling so rapidly when it is applied locally.

A healthy cat was given ether in order to observe the difference between this and other types of anaesthetics. Without having known it previously, DVK stated correctly that the cat was normal in every way. After fifteen minutes, the flow of etheric energy in the body began to slow down; after another twenty minutes, the energy was seen to resume its normal flow, and subsequently the front legs of the cat began to move. She was able to walk soon thereafter.

When the anaesthetic Pentothol was injected intravenously, the etheric was pushed out of the animal's body and became localized above the head more rapidly than in the case of ether. Some connections within the physical body remained, however. This observation explains the effectiveness of Pentothol for human use, for the loss of consciousness is swift and pleasant.

Sandy, a four-year-old Sheltie, was to undergo spaying, and a dose of four grains of Pentothol was slowly injected intravenously. DVK noted that "the drug dulls the etheric brain's response and slows its energy pattern, and at the same time there is generalized dulling of the etheric all over the body." After a few minutes, the dog began to receive metophane gas by inhalation. In consequence, the etheric around the head became still duller, and there was a slight loosening of its contact with the physical body. Within five minutes the etheric became even less bright and was pushed farther towards the head. Everything in the physical body seemed to slow down.

Before the dog's abdomen was opened, DVK reported that the right ovary was slightly larger than the left. Dr. Weule began the surgery by cutting the skin of the abdomen to remove the dog's uterus and ovaries. When he reached the ovaries, he confirmed DVK's observation that the right ovary was slightly larger and more cystic than the left.

At the moment of cutting the uterus and the right ovary, DVK noted that the pattern of the etheric was also being cut, and that the flow of etheric energy to the area discontinued. The cut portions became duller and very low in vitality. The left ovary was then removed.

After the excision, the anaesthesia was diminished. The etheric pattern of the ovaries and uterus which had been removed changed rapidly, first becoming dimmer, then diminishing, and vanishing within a short time.

In about half an hour, when the abdomen was being sutured, DVK observed that the internal organs of the dog began to compensate immediately, and that channels or lines of etheric energy began to form new circuits where the uterus and ovaries had been removed. This is similar to the pattern we see medically, when the blood supply is cut or obstructed and new vascular channels begin to form—but this process takes much longer.

Continued observation of the dog's etheric brain showed that its brightness was returning slowly as the anaesthesia wore off. It was noted that the etheric pattern in dogs is much simpler than in humans: it dies down more quickly, but it also comes together more quickly, as when the suturing was done. This helps to explain why animals recover more rapidly than we do. After one hour the etheric pattern of the excised area began to reestablish itself; the etheric mesh was tightening, indicating that the healing process was proceeding rapidly. In contrast, the etheric counterpart of the two organs that were removed was fast diminishing and became practically nonexistent in an hour.

In another case, DVK observed a German shepherd dog that had been sick for three weeks. She noticed that the animal was trying to fight off an infection. Vitality was low, the kidneys were not functioning well, and the dog was in pain. The solar plexus chakra was very much disturbed and out of function, producing painful spasms. The etheric was thin in this area.

Looking at a third animal that seemed very ill, DVK predicted that it would not survive because the etheric was decreasing in vitality and loosening from the physical body as if under anaesthetic. This indicated to her that death was imminent, which was later confirmed by the veterinarian.

5
The Role of
Consciousness

XV
The Effects of
Changes in Consciousness

In the research DVK and I did together many years ago, the emphasis was upon the chakras and their influence on the disease process, and consciousness was rarely mentioned. Nevertheless both of us recognized that consciousness is a basic factor in self-actualization and self-transformation, and this, of course, is reflected in the chakras. These can and do change in response to modifications in our thinking and feeling, as well as in our patterns of behavior, and this change in turn affects the healing process.

In the chapters that follow we have tried to describe the effect of the ways we feel and think about our health. All of us are conscious beings, and our choices and the actions that stem from them are part of this aspect of our nature, whether we are aware of it or not.

Meditation and Visualization

One of the ways in which we become aware of our own inner nature is through meditation. Meditation is a conscious effort to withdraw our focus of attention from the immediate physical and emotional distractions which we all experience in daily life, and to center it within. Through such centering we gain a sense of unity with higher dimensions of the self, and this becomes a great source of strength and peace.

There are many different meditation techniques which achieve the same results. The important element is regularity, for without this there can be little long-term effect. Habitual practice builds up confidence and establishes a harmonious link between all the levels of consciousness which we have described. If practiced daily, meditation can alter habits which create tension and can make a definite change in the personality and health of the individual. This is reflected in the chakras, as their rhythm will alter and new energy will flow in, thus helping to break destructive habit patterns. The chakras will begin to function together in harmony, and this in turn brings additional energy into the whole system. Even if one is tired when sitting down to meditate at the end of the day, one feels not only relaxed but energized afterwards.

In many cases, meditation gives a sense of self-mastery, so that a person feels able to change old habit patterns. It is through so doing that meditation can help us overcome the disease process.

One of DVK's personal observations over the years—during which she has focused her attention primarily on the effects of healing and to a lesser extent on the functioning of the chakras—is that meditation has a therapeutic effect. The sense of being part of a greater whole helps us to free ourselves from the common delusion that we are the center of everything, and from being preoccupied with ourselves. This feeling of wholeness also abates our tendency to concentrate on our illness—a tendency which only reinforces the disease process. Instead of identifying ourselves with our illness, we become aware of our own state of mind and of our ability to change it.

It has been found that under stress the whole body is thrown into strain, and that the sympathetic nervous system is activated by the mere thought of something that must be escaped or dealt with forcibly. Heartbeat and breath become faster, adrenalin pours into the system, and the person may sweat. That all this can take place when something frightening appears in the imagination shows that there is no boundary between the physical body and the thoughts and feelings; what we imagine can be terrifyingly real to us.

In the same way, imagining or visualizing happy and peaceful situations can have a tranquilizing effect. Visualization can certainly be very useful, for it helps to strengthen the power of concentration. For example, if we are anxious we should focus upon whatever is to us a symbol of peace, and visualize this not only during meditation but also during the day whenever anxiety begins to arise in us. If a symbol is to be effective, it must have meaning for us; therefore a person should select one that is connected with his own personal experience.

To DVK, one of the most effective symbols is a tree, which is rooted in the earth, reaches out to the sun for its life sustenance, and is constantly buffeted by wind and weather. In all cultures the sun is a symbol of spiritual reality, and the weather represents the changing circumstances of our daily life; thus the tree not only has immediate personal meaning for us in terms of our experience of nature, but also stands for the possibility of our "weathering" our day-to-day problems and of becoming more aware of that spiritual dimension which persists through all personal storms.

When we visualize, we are using the power of the brow chakra, and this shows up clearly to clairvoyant sight, since it not only speeds up the rotation of this center but also affects the crown chakra. Therefore the practice of positive visualization helps to promote the healing process, for it energizes the whole system and thus can have a beneficent effect on our health.

The greatest energy can be drawn from the highest levels of our consciousness. We can awaken to these levels within us through prayer and meditation, and also by truly altruistic actions. Genuine altruism breaks the pattern of self-concern, which often is the cause of somatic illness.

Meditation can lead to an indestructible conviction

that we can be whole, because we participate in the wholeness of the universe itself. When we are centered, there is no feeling of being caught in the disorder that may be around us, and thus we can experience real peace. This builds an inner core of steadiness which can keep us serene and in balance even in the face of life's difficulties.

A case of great interest to DVK illustrates the effects both upon the chakras and on the healing process when changes in consciousness occur. A young woman who had a severe case of rheumatoid arthritis also had very little confidence in herself and her own abilities. At the time she came to see us, her energy system was low, and this of course affected her chakras. Soon thereafter she became very much interested both in meditation and in the healing process, and began the regular practice of meditation.

This made a great difference in her general health, and her chakra system reflected the change. Several of her centers were particularly affected: the brow chakra, the seat of concentration, and the crown chakra, the seat of consciousness and the gateway of higher energies, began to act in harmony with each other and with the heart chakra, and this in turn influenced the functioning of the solar plexus chakra. By consciously changing her thought patterns, she transferred her focus from the solar plexus to the heart, and this transformed the whole system.

When the heart and crown chakras work together harmoniously, this acts upon the thymus gland and strengthens the immune system. At the same time that this was taking place in this patient, she tried to involve herself in helping others through healing, which also brought new energy into the heart chakra. There was a noticeable change in both the rhythm and the movement of her three higher centers.

All this dramatically changed her life. In a few years the arthritis disappeared, and the integration of her faculties gave her self-confidence. She was able to take on a responsible position in important and difficult welfare work, which strengthened her recognition that she could make a contribution to others and her determination to lead a life of altruism.

The regular practice of meditation relaxes tension as well as focusing the mind on a lofty or universal concept. This is liberating because it reaches a level beyond the problems and desires of the personal self. This changes the energy in the crown chakra and opens the mind and heart to dimensions of consciousness which flood one with peace, reduce emotional stress, and thus affect the whole body.

Higher Sense Perception

Ever since childhood, VPN had been aware of her ability to perceive objects at a distance and communicate telepathically with nonphysical beings. On one occasion when she was about seven years old, she saw a playmate being accidentally killed by a train. When VPN rushed to her mother in great distress and described the accident, she was reprimanded for concocting such a terrible story, for her friend lived more than a hundred miles away. In a few days they received news that the child was dead, and VPN's vision was verified. But she had learned a lesson and kept such experiences to herself until later in life.

DVK knew nothing about these paranormal experiences during VPN's childhood. Nevertheless, when asked to evaluate her chakras, DVK described changes in the crown and brow chakras as well as the pineal and pituitary glands, all indicating that VPN had telepathic abilities as well as spiritual awareness. The details of the case are given in the appendix, but here we note that the changes observed in both the crown and brow chakras were related especially to the degree of luminosity, the rate of motion, the size and the elasticity, all of which were above normal. The pineal gland was functioning at a rate above average, being stimulated by the crown chakra, which was closely connected to the brow center.

The indications of paranormal abilities revealed by the chakras were corroborated by observation of her mental body, whose size and brightness confirmed her telepathic ability, and indicated the presence of an inflow from higher dimensions of consciousness, which gave her a kind of intuitive "knowing."

DVK also pointed out which of the etheric centers and their corresponding endocrine glands might give the subject future physical problems. Twenty years later, VPN developed symptoms which confirmed this prediction.

These and other observations indicate that the chakras are affected by our thoughts and feelings, and that they are part of the mechanism which connects our physical body to the subtler elements of our nature. Thus they are elements in the process of spiritual growth.

XVI
The Dynamics of Healing

Any study of the disease process must have as its goal an increase in our understanding of the factors which lead to healing and the reestablishment of health and well-being. Healing in this sense goes beyond the cure of a specific illness, and means the restoration of wholeness, which the disease process disrupts. Today it is widely recognized that healing in this regenerative sense is self-engendered. The process can and usually must be medically assisted in order to remove the obstacles to cure, but in the final analysis the body must heal itself.

Nevertheless, the healing process is still full of mystery. How do spontaneous remissions occur? Why do some people recover completely from very severe illnesses, while others succumb in spite of the most skillful treatment? Our investigations bear upon these questions significantly, since they point to the fact that the fields and the chakras play an important role in the maintenance of health and in the complexity of the body's immune and other systems. Thus our observations can help us understand how and when healing takes place, and why it does not.

It is within the mystery of human nature that the causes of health and disease are to be found. In the East it is said that we reap only the fruits of our past and present action. The past is beyond changing, but its results remain with us for better or worse. The future is unpredictable, yet its seeds lie in the present—and about the present we *can* do something. What we do, what we eat and drink, what we feel and think—our habits and behavior—all constantly contribute to what we are now and what we will be tomorrow. But this picture is not cast in concrete. Like everything else in nature, human life is a dynamic process, and thus we all have the ability to alter our patterns of behavior, and thereby change ourselves and our futures.

All of the observations which DVK has made indicate that health and healing are dependent upon a natural, harmonic, unimpeded flow of life energy. As previously described, this energy is a universal field force, and thus always present, but its flow can be curtailed or inhibited under certain conditions. Equally, its flow can be enhanced, and this is the principle which underlies the dynamics of all healing done without medical intervention, whether it be called spiritual healing, therapeutic touch, natural healing or by any other name. Some of the factors which contribute to this enhancement have been known for a long time; others are more mysterious.

For example, DVK visited the city of Varanasi (Benares) in India, long held to be most holy, where thousands of people come every day to bathe in the cleansing waters of the Ganges and be purified by its healing powers. Looked at with our physical eyes, and having in mind the usual Western notions of hygiene, the city is very dirty and the river ought to be heavily polluted by the numbers of sick and dying and dead who are immersed in its waters. Yet looked at etherically it presents a different picture.

Normally, every river or moving body of water has a very slight etheric counterpart which extends about three inches above the surface. The Ganges is no exception for most of its course. However, at the point in Varanasi where pilgrims enter the river, DVK observed what she described as a condition of "double-decker etheric energy" extending perhaps half a mile along the banks, but not found farther upstream or downstream. Along this stretch of the river there was a special flow of etheric energy extending about one inch under the surface of the water. In addition, about a mile upstream from this point there was another concentration of energy, which might almost be called a spiritual vortex of healing energies. (These occur all over the world.)

It is strange but true that for many healing does take place in this part of the river. DVK's explanation is that, because of its special conditions, when the patient dips into the waters of the Ganges at this spot he receives enough extra etheric energy to effect a quicker recovery than would be normally the case.

"Miraculous" Cures

On occasion especially sensitive people can spontaneously draw upon healing forces in nature, in order to concentrate energy and effect cures. Kathryn Kuhlman (1907-1976) was one such. All her healing was done in a religious setting in the presence of as many as seven thousand people who participated in the service, thus adding their energy to the process. Her healings were always spontaneous and dramatic, and their efficacy was confirmed by physicians time and time again. In her weekly television program she presented the patients who claimed to have been healed, along with medical reports that verified their statements, or the physicians themselves.

We attended two of Kathryn Kuhlman's healing services in May, 1970, and January, 1974. On both of these occasions the procedures were identical. The services lasted from 1:00 to 5:00 P.M., and we arrived an hour early so that DVK could observe Miss Kuhlman both before and during the healing service.

At both of these services there was organ music and a choir of over two hundred voices which sang hymns. DVK's opinion was that the rhythm and vigor of the music played an important part in preparing for the healing, by building a tremendous thought-form which enveloped the whole auditorium and united the energies of the thousands of people present.

As a rule, Kathryn Kuhlman came on stage an hour before the service was to begin and joined in singing with the choir. In this instance, DVK observed that the healer's astral and etheric fields were very bright, and that they had an unusual ability to expand enormously so as to envelop a very large area. Her chakras were bright and fast moving, and the whole chakra system, including the astral and mental levels, was harmonious, synchronized and well integrated. During the service she was sensitized to an outstanding degree.

Throughout the healing service itself, DVK noted that as the organ was playing a rainbow-hued pattern of color began to envelop the whole auditorium, and that this pattern was reproduced in the musical form created by the organ, which was an important factor in the whole process. Together, these patterns engendered a pulsating flood of light and color which seemed to center on or emanate from the platform where Kathryn Kuhlman stood.

Observing the healer's chakras, DVK noticed that the solar plexus, the brow and the crown chakras were the most powerful, and that there was a state of almost perfect harmony between the etheric and astral centers. There were no blocks. When Miss Kuhlman prayed, she tuned into the tremendous spiritual power which she called God, and she became for the time its focus and channel.

As the service progressed, the concerted force of the prayers and singing focused and consolidated a link with the healing forces. The unity of the immense audience enabled Miss Kuhlman to draw on some of its etheric energy in order to help her build up a condition of enormous power. This energy was both etheric and astral. As she began to talk about the Holy Spirit, she became tremendously charged with energy, and all her vehicles (that is, her aura) began to stretch and expand. She became like a great electrical dynamo, or a lightning rod which attracted this higher force. When she started to speak with deep conviction her face became pale, and DVK believed she was not fully conscious of what was happening, although she was aware she was being used as a channel by a force beyond herself. She constantly repeated that she herself was not the healer but rather the Holy Spirit, of which she was the instrument.

One of the most interesting aspects of her healing was that Miss Kuhlman did not know who was to be healed and could not choose the candidates for help. She would seemingly become aware during the process itself, either from a feeling which went through her or a sense of "hearing" what the problem was, or perhaps an emotional rapport with the person and disease being healed at that moment. She would point to the spot in the auditorium where healing was taking place and identify the part of the body in the person, such as spine or lungs. She seldom mentioned the specific disease, although sometimes she would say "cancer."

At the moment of healing, the patients felt a tremendous stream of energy passing through them, which many described as "a bolt of lightning," coming from a deep spiritual level right through the emotional and etheric fields. The solar plexus and crown chakras were the two most affected. The "bolt of lightning" sensation came when these two and then all the other chakras were speeded up.

This speeding up was accomplished by the help of higher-level forces.[1] It affected the body's metabolism to such an extent that the proper balance was achieved instantaneously and persisted after the service ended. The patients invariably felt a tremendous heat passing through their bodies, to such a degree that it was sometimes palpable to those sitting beside them.

According to DVK, it was this sudden speeding up of

---

1. Traditionally in spiritual healing, the healers have drawn upon or acknowledged the presence of forces working through them, which they identify with God, angels or other spiritual beings.

the chakra system that checked the disease process. Those who were healed were told to throw away their braces and crutches and walk up to the platform in order to test what had happened. Kathryn Kuhlman would touch the patients' foreheads with her fingers, and the impact of such touching was so great that it usually made the patients fall over backward. She called this being "slain with the power." This blessing was extremely potent. Through it the patients were given an added charge, which helped to "lock" the healing energy into their systems so that it would continue to work in them for some time. The force in Kuhlman's hands was so strong on occasion that it not only knocked down the person being healed but also a number of other people standing nearby, who toppled over like a row of dominoes.

Kathryn Kuhlman was undoubtedly a unique healer, with the ability to tap spiritual energies of great power. One of the mysteries of her healing was that she herself had no control over which patients would be chosen for cure. DVK felt that it was the karma[2] of the individual patient that determined who would be healed. Certainly this had nothing to do with believing in Kuhlman's ability or in being a member of the Christian faith, for many skeptics and nonbelievers were healed in spite of themselves.

There was a question in DVK's mind, however, as to whether the experience of being healed would change a person in the long run, and whether it might make one more sensitive to the needs of others. She had an opportunity to observe a patient with rheumatoid arthritis who had been healed by Kuhlman the year before, and noticed that a tiny link had been made between the person's higher or spiritual level and the emotions. It was as though the healing energy had penetrated the astral body, and this had effected a real and enduring change in the person.

It is spiritual energy that produces a transformation of emotional patterns, and this can create a lasting change

2. The consequences of past actions.

in the astral body. For the patients, the experience was one of complete joy, and in consequence many of them became warmer and more open in their relationships with others.

Healers as Transmitters of Etheric Energy

Practitioners who use their hands in healing are to be found all over the world and in every walk of life; they may be physicians, ministers, chiropractors, nurses or lay persons. Many of them discover their ability accidentally and some cannot at first believe that everyone does not share these powers.

This kind of healing, which was frequently referred to as magnetic healing in the past, now includes the modality known as Therapeutic Touch. There are many individual variations in the method, but all who practice it say they feel some sensations in the hands. The most common is a sense of heat, which fluctuates in accordance with the patient's needs. It may be accompanied by other sensations, either simultaneously or consecutively: a pulse in the palms, a feeling of coolness, a sense of drawing or constriction, a needle-like tingling, a prickly, crackling sensation, the sensation of a lump in the palm, and even a sharp pain in the hands or arms. Some report that their hands are attracted to a spot they sense as being the cause of the difficulty, rather than to the area which the patient identifies as painful. Most healers are aware when the flow of energy commences, and when it ceases.

Most patients, on the other hand, feel an increased sense of relaxation and well-being when they are being treated by a healer. A few describe a generalized or sometimes a local sense of heat when being treated. There may at times be sharp, aching, tingling waves of pain flowing from the affected parts through the hands or feet; this may be felt as a burning sensation, as prickly, as flowing in rivulets, or merely as a sense of pressure.

The attitude of the patient towards the healing process does not affect its efficacy. As mentioned above, some who attended Kathryn Kuhlman's meetings came out of curiosity and were healed without having asked for or expected it. Nor can the healer's desire to cure the patient control the healing process.

The duration of the treatment varies according to the need and the response of the patient, and this is transmitted to the healer's awareness through his hands. It may last a few minutes or half an hour. Relief of pain may occur immediately, but symptoms may recur within a few hours or days, and therefore the treatment may have to be repeated several times. Occasionally there is a temporary exacerbation of the symptoms for a few hours or days before the healing takes effect.

Some healers seem to have an "automatic thermostat" within them which shuts off the flow of etheric energy at the appropriate time. In such cases there is rarely any danger of overloading the patient. However, when healers are overenthusiastic and do not pay attention to their inner cues, they may pour too much energy into a patient with distressing and even harmful effects.

From the above, the reader will gather that we perceive that healing takes different forms and is uneven in its effects, because of many unknown factors, both in the patients and in the process. Most healers who use Therapeutic Touch or similar methods do increase the flow of energy in the patients and remove blockages. This may or may not be enough to set the healing process going within the patients, and thus achieve a lasting effect. The kind of healing which is accomplished by a person who is naturally gifted, or that takes place under seemingly "miraculous" circumstances, is remarkable in that the effects are felt immediately and the results are long-lasting.

Observations of Other Healers

Frances Farrelly (whose identity can be disclosed since she herself has already revealed it) was the sensitive called Kay in SK's book *Breakthrough to Creativity*. She has numerous psychic abilities, some of which are more highly developed than others. She is very sensitive, and can feel a person's physical or emotional state. It was she who first called SK's attention to what we called "sappers," that is, people who draw upon the etheric or emotional energies of others and thus devitalize them. She is a good magnetic healer, but has no control over the results of her healing. At times she is a good psychometrist, but her real forte is dowsing for water, minerals, archaeological remains, lost objects or lost persons. She also has good control over the expansion or contraction of her etheric fingers.

Since early childhood, FF has been aware of the presence of nature spirits, but her clairvoyance is sporadic and limited. She is unable to see the chakras. She can occasionally see and influence objects at a distance, and has had a few outstanding precognitive experiences. She is objective in her research, flexible in her ideas, humorous in temperament, and always ready to explore new ideas in her search for truth.

When studying the work of healers, one must observe them while they are at work. In one of our many experiments together, FF states that when healing begins her hands become hot, and when the healing is completed the heat disappears automatically. We asked DVK to observe what happens during this process. The patient was suffering from an upper respiratory infection and sore throat. FF was asked to heal her, and she and the patient sat about fifteen feet away from DVK and SK. Healing began within a few moments after FF placed her right hand over the throat of the patient. DVK observed that the healer generated a flow of etheric energy from her head to her hands, which then played between her hands through the throat area of the patient she was treating. The right hand appeared the more sensitive of the two. The sensation of heat in the hands of the healer appears to clairvoyant observation as an orange-red color emanating from her fingertips.

In this experiment, the heat felt by FF was observed by DVK a few moments before it became apparent either to the healer or the patient. (DVK's observations were noted silently, and neither patient nor healer knew of them at the time.) The color orange-red indicated that the energy was flowing; as it changed to yellow the energy diminished.

We tested FF's claim that she could both charge a person with etheric energy or drain it away. She sat facing the subject, and DVK and SK sat fifteen feet away. FF focused her eyes on the subject's eyes, and in a few minutes DVK reported that she was pulling energy out. DVK then asked FF to reverse the process and charge the subject with etheric energy, which she did. After several repetitions of the experiment, we concluded that FF did have the ability to energize or devitalize. Later we studied subjects who "sapped" astral and mental energies as well as the etheric.

The ability of people to heal themselves varies tremendously, and even the most famous healers have died of natural causes. Nevertheless, they can on occasion effect a self-cure. About twenty-five years ago FF mentioned a complaint to SK, who recognized the problem as a mass in the descending colon which was probably cancerous. This was confirmed by DVK, who observed an obstruction in the area's energy flow. FF was referred to a physician, and was diagnosed as having a malignant growth which required surgery.

FF, however, was convinced that her disease was partly emotional in origin, and she decided that she must resolve this problem before taking any other action. She spent the next two or three years meditating and facing her emotional problems squarely. The cancer receded, the mass began to diminish, and she has been well for the last twenty-two years. Although this method is certainly not recommended for everyone, FF was able to heal herself by changing her emotional patterns. (Permission has been given us to report this case.)

Several other healers were observed at work by DVK. In general, their etheric fields tended to be somewhat more luminous and sometimes larger than the average.

The chakras were also unusually luminous and elastic. These characteristics seem to be common to healers, even though they may differ considerably in their methods. In some cases the brow and throat chakras appeared to be larger than average. (Case histories of three healers will be found in the appendix.)

The Case of Colonel Estabany

Colonel Oskar Estabany discovered his healing ability in a most unusual way. An officer in the Hungarian cavalry, he was much attached to his horse. The animal had the misfortune to break its leg, and as this is usually fatal in such animals, the decision was made to destroy it. Col. Estabany went into the stall where the horse was lying in order to say good-bye to it, and he began to run his hand soothingly over the injured leg. After he had done this for some time, the horse began to move around, heaved itself on to its feet and finally was able to walk. This seemed such an impossible feat for a horse with a broken leg, that it was reexamined, and it was found that the leg had completely mended.

After this experience, Col. Estabany ventured to practice healing on people, and found that he could help them as well. Later he emigrated to Canada, where his healing ability was evaluated first by Dr. Bernard Grad of McGill University, and later by Sister Justa Smith of Buffalo, New York. Dr. Grad reported that Col. Estabany was able to cause burns in mice to heal much more rapidly than the norm. He also accelerated the growth of seeds by sprinkling them with water that he held in his hands for half an hour.

The experiments with Col. Estabany which were conducted by Sister Justa Smith were widely written up and became very well known. (See Chapter VII.) She asked him to restore to normalcy the activity of an enzyme (trypsinogen) that had been damaged, which he did successfully, although further studies conducted by Sister Justa found that very few healers could duplicate his results. This raised the question as to whether some healers are more effective in treating certain types of diseases than others because of factors in their own etheric and astral fields. These factors could perhaps be specified, in which case healers could specialize in certain diseases according to their abilities.

Later, DVK collaborated with Col. Estabany in his healing work and was able to observe how the energy exchange took place. From this she realized that others could learn to effect similar beneficial results through conscious intervention, even though they might not be natural healers like Col. Estabany. This resulted in the development of the healing method called Therapeutic Touch, in which Dr. Dolores Krieger and DVK were closely associated.

Thus, although the study of healers and the healing process may have been somewhat peripheral to the original purpose of this book, it could be said that our investigations have assisted in opening up the field of healing more widely to health practitioners. Since the time we did this research, DVK herself has steadily pursued the study of the etheric field and the chakras and has applied her knowledge to the development of more re-fined techniques for Therapeutic Touch. This in turn has helped a large number of sick patients. Clinical studies have shown over and over again that the etheric energy which was the subject of our investigations does perform a real function in health and disease, and that it is possible to remove blockages to the flow of this energy by conscious intervention. Therefore, there have been some practical results of our study which go far beyond what we en-visioned at the time.

XVII
Towards the Future

PART ONE BY SHAFICA KARAGULLA

In this book, we have offered data obtained by clairvoyant observation that may take us one step further in unravelling the complex problem of health and human wholeness. Whether or not our material is fully accepted, it should at least raise important questions for future investigation. The most significant of these, from our point of view, relate to the nature of what we have called etheric energy, the mechanisms which regulate its renewal and depletion (the chakras), and how these affect physical function and the maintenance of good health.

Even if our premises are not yet accepted by the medical profession, they are being reinforced every day by a growing recognition that the physical systems within the body are regulated by processes which are so refined as to be well-nigh "nonphysical" in the ordinary sense of the term. Our postulation of other energy fields which are subtler than those so far measured, but which impinge upon the physical world, is consistent with contemporary knowledge; the notion that these subtle energies are related to different states of consciousness is more revolutionary, but not incompatible with the position of scientists who theorize that mind is a concomitant of matter.

As we look toward the future, what can be concluded from the work that DVK and I have done together? Before identifying what seems most significant to us, it should be acknowledged that some of our data is inconclusive. Knowing this, we present it anyway, hoping to stimulate readers and other researchers to think of health and disease in new terms. Another point to be mentioned is that we did not always totally agree in our points of view. We have differed about the role and importance of some of the chakras, for example. I chose the direction of the research, focusing primarily on the mechanism of the centers, whereas to DVK it is the relation between the energy field and the chakras that is important for diagnosis. In spite of some differences in our priorities, however, we always worked together very harmoniously.

The first significant observation we made was that a dissonance—that is, a disease process—may exist for many years on the etheric, astral or mental levels before it manifests physically. DVK would point out the areas of weakness, and her observations were confirmed in those cases which we were able to follow up over a period of time.

A second important point was that the excision of a diseased endocrine gland, such as the thyroid, did not at once cure the abnormality in the chakra. We conclude from this that, in order to effect permanent healing, we must discover how to treat the condition in the chakra. Such a challenge obviously requires a two-step approach: first, the researcher must acknowledge that the problem has a deep-seated source (whether or not identified as a chakra by name), and second, he must find out the ways to cure it. So far, no one has even begun to discover how to treat the etheric chakras, although there are some who make ridiculous claims that they are able to "open" or "close" a chakra—claims which are quite unsubstantiated. Most healers do not make the attempt, and fortunately it is not easy to affect the centers, although many can increase the vitality of the patient, remove blockages and relieve pain, thus enhancing the healing process.

Third, it should be reemphasized that we could not determine which part of the body would be affected by the abnormal functioning of a particular chakra. For example, if the throat center was affected, we were unable to tell whether it would result in disease of the thyroid, lungs or breast.

Fourth, DVK's observations offer clues to the nature of higher sense perception and the possibility of its development. There is intense interest in this field at present, and a large number of people are claiming various degrees of ability. The *testing* of such claims, however, is practically nonexistent. As our work demonstrates, it is fairly easy to devise methods of research which would prove or disprove the validity of any person's higher sense perception.

The question of its development is much more difficult. DVK has identified some of the requirements, but there are many unknowns. There are, in fact, dangers in this field, as would be the case in any science that is not adequately understood. It is our position that clairvoyant investigation should come under the domain of science, since its area of research includes types of energy and their effect upon physical states, and therefore it should be pursued with the same degree of care and control as any other scientific project. (Unfortunately, many of those who have higher sense perception refuse to submit to such testing, and wish their observations to be taken at face value.) Just as Madame Curie suffered severe burns because of her ignorance of radioactivity, so the person who explores new fields of consciousness and energy puts himself in jeopardy unless he is thoroughly familiar with what is so far known.

Other questions arise, not so much from our research as from the concepts about man which form its context. For example, based upon the hypothesis that the human personality is a triune phenomenon, is this triplicity reflected on the physical level? The physical body is itself composed of a triad of three types of cells which arise after the union of the ovum and the sperm, known embryologically as the endoderm (inner layer), the mesoderm (middle layer) and the ectoderm (outer layer). Different endocrine glands may arise from any one of the three embryological layers, i.e.: the thyroid from the endoderm, the gonads from the mesoderm, the pituitary from the ectoderm. I have often wondered what role these three basic cell types play, not only in the incidence of disease, but also in the therapeutic approach to healing. In future we may study the type of cell structure from which the disease arises, rather than merely its symptoms.

An important concept which emerges from our research, and has been emphasized in case after case, is that of dissonance. We have spoken of the harmonic system of the chakras; the idea that a pattern of harmonic relationship exists not only in the chakras but throughout nature is one that is almost limitless in its implications. It points toward a universe whose laws are based on mathematical and musical, rather than mechanical, principles. When we apply these to the study of a human being, we perceive that health is a harmonic process of delicate but powerful interactions and interrelationships among the various levels of body, emotions, mind and spirit which together constitute the creature that is man.

What are the factors that contribute to a condition of inner harmony? The concept that there are three fields of the personality, or the personal self, implies that each of these is indispensable, and that damage at any level results in physical impairment or disease. But even when undamaged, if one of these fields is out of harmony or balance with the rest, the results will be apparent. Therefore, a state of health or well-being means that these three fields must not only function freely on their own level but must also resonate together in harmony with each other and with the physical organism as well. We can then speak of disease as a state of being "out of tune," as Pythagoras argued. Applying this idea to the chakra system, if one center is overstimulated while another is underactive, the harmonious balance is disturbed, and the system as a whole becomes "dissonant."

Another concept which our research has reinforced is that disease occurs only within the three fields of the personality, and that holistic medicine is technically engaged with "personal wholeness." The true self or soul of man remains whole even when the body suffers illness, and healing takes place when that wholeness is reestablished at all levels. This is a revolutionary concept that will require a dramatic shift in our perception of health and of the role of medicine.

We believe that tomorrow's therapeutic approach will move away from total reliance on drugs and chemicals, towards the use of subtler techniques which engage the patient's own resources. Some of these are already being drawn upon in retraining the body and bringing brain patterns under conscious control. Once medicine fully accepts the human potential for self-renewal, many new techniques will undoubtedly be developed.

Some of these techniques will be directed at establishing healthy mental and emotional patterns, just as habits of proper diet and exercise are emphasized today in order to prevent future disease. What are the attitudes which promote health? We know a great deal about the damage created by stress and by negative feelings of fear, anxiety and resentment. Should we not extend the idea of preventive medicine to include the conscious development of positive emotions such as love and sympathy, which induce inner peace and harmony? Is it possible that even serious social problems, such as drug addiction, could be approached from the point of view of trying to reestablish a state of balance and wholeness within the patient?

The reader will undoubtedly agree that our investigations open up more questions than they answer. But the ability to ask the right questions is the key to successful research. If the most challenging problem that faces us today is mankind itself, then we need to be daring and look everywhere for clues, even in directions which have heretofore been closed to us—sometimes by ignorance, sometimes by prejudice.

The next step belongs to the future.

Part Two by Dora van Gelder Kunz

To close this account of the investigations in which I participated with Dr. Karagulla, I should like to sum up what I perceive as the results of the research, in the light of what I have learned from the twenty years of work in healing which I have done subsequently. During this time I have gained a somewhat different perspective on the chakras and their functions, but I could not incorporate many of these ideas in the book itself, since this is primarily concerned with the work I did jointly with Dr. Karagulla.

Dr. Karagulla was mainly interested in the phenomenon of clairvoyance as revealed in the data of pure observation, and the correlation of such data with those of medical diagnoses. I am forced to say that at no time has this been my primary interest, which was then, and still remains, healing and the establishment of health and wholeness in the patient. Thus I have for some time been engaged with the teaching and practice of Therapeutic Touch as a healing technique accessible to health professionals, especially by contributing my observations of what happens in sickness and how the healing process can be enhanced.

The chakras are centers of energy which are constantly interacting with one another from hour to hour, and changes in the energy patterns occur as a continuing process. Healing is therefore reflected in changes of rhythm and other basic alterations in these centers.

Meditation and visualization, if done regularly and combined with changes in behavior, can produce modifications in the chakra patterns, and these are reflected in the person's health and physical well-being. A genuine transformation can thus be observed. Whether the person knows about the role the chakras play as energy centers makes no difference whatsoever.

At the moment, general interest in the chakras is growing. In the last few years, several books have been published on the subject, some of them written by doctors who include the chakras in surveys dealing with general health. In the future, I believe this interest will increase to the extent that the chakra system may become a subject for medical research.

As for myself, I am at present engaged in writing a book in which I hope to describe in greater detail the properties of the astral world and the important part the chakras play in the healing process. The study to which Dr. Karagulla devoted so much of her time and energy will, I feel sure, be a useful introduction to future research, in which I hope many more of the medical profession will be engaged.

Appendix
CASE HISTORIES

The Crown Chakra

The Case of CT

The General Field

Color   Bluish gray with patches of gray scattered throughout. Darker shades of gray around head.

Luminosity   Above average, but dull in parts.

Movement   Average in speed, but slow around the head. There was both a rhythmic and dysrhythmic pattern.

Size   Wider than average, but not symmetrical. Right side wider, but droopy. Thicker etheric on the right side of head. Etheric broken into fine granules on the left side of head.

Elasticity   Excellent prior to hemiplegia. Some blockage. Right hand showed longer etheric fingers. Poor elasticity on top of the head.

Texture   Fine. Thick on the right side of the head, broken on the left side of the head.

Function: Right hand etheric fingers about 15 centimeters in length, indicating sensitivity in the hand with a potential for healing. Granulation of the etheric on the left side of the head indicated damage to brain. The etheric was thicker on the right side of the head. There were many patches of gray scattered throughout the etheric field, with local blockages. There was a great deal of cholesterol in the arteries of the brain and heart.

Correlation: There was excellent correlation between DVK's description and the medical condition. The basic damage was assessed by the granulation of the etheric, and observed to be on the left side of the brain. The etheric on the right paralyzed side was droopy, which was a perfect anatomical description of where the damage was.

The Etheric Crown Chakra

Characteristics	Petals	Core
Color	Golden blue	Dark blue
Luminosity	Bright	Dull
Rhythm	Dysrhythmic	Dysrhythmic
Rate	Fast but fluctuating	Slow
Size	Larger than average	Larger than average
Form	Petals down; not sharp	Break on left side
Elasticity	Excellent	Poor
Texture	Fine	Loose

Function: This chakra is abnormal. There is great discrepancy between the petals and the core. The luminosity of the petals gives evidence of meditation. The core indicates a disease process giving rise to aphasia and right hemiplegia.

About six centimeters above the core of the crown chakra there was an area that showed decreased energy on the left side.

Pineal Gland: Developed and functioning.

Correlation: Excellent correlation between the etheric crown center and the medical condition of the patient.

DVK's description of what she perceived etherically in the brain was interesting. She stated that part of the brain which seems to deal with the mechanism of hearing is what she thinks of as the "sounding board." The electrical impulses which normally act as the sounding board are damaged. This in turn interferes with the mechanism of hearing. The "monitor of speech" within the etheric brain is gone. There is also dysrhythmia, with slowing of energy in the frontal lobes. The posterior part of the brain shows jagged frontal energy compared to the frontal lobes. The area of decreased energy on the left side above the core of the chakra was probably due to the damage on the left side of the brain.

The Etheric Brow Chakra

Characteristics	Petals	Core
Color	Reddish blue	Alternating yellow/red
Luminosity	Above average	Fluctuating from good average to dull
Rhythm	Dysrhythmic	Dysrhythmic
Rate	More than average	Less than average
Size	Normal	Normal
Form	Normal, but slightly down	Deviated, not sharp
Elasticity	Above average	Less than average
Texture	Fine	Thick

Function: The chakra is abnormal in its function.

Pituitary Gland: This has been affected. Overfunctioning of the adrenals was observed, which in turn seemed to affect the blood. There was some "thickening" of the blood, which might have contributed to his stroke.

This patient has had some psychic ability, such as seeing visions, but this has been damaged by his illness.

Correlation: Good.

The Etheric Solar Plexus Chakra

Characteristics	Petals	Core
Color	Green and orange/red, but muddy	Green, but muddy
Luminosity	Above average	Below average
Rhythm	Variable	Variable

Rate	Above average	Above average
Size	Larger than average	Larger than average
Form	Larger, curved up	Larger, leakage
Elasticity	Above average	Above average
Texture	Fine	Thick

Function: This chakra deviated from normal, as indicated by the muddiness of the colors and the dysrhythmia. The core indicated slow recuperative powers. The center had been used in his work as a healer. It was also the center through which he became depleted and exhausted.

Note: Additional cases in which the crown chakra is involved may be found in "Diseases Related to Consciousness and the Brain," Chapter XII.

The Case of VC: Epilepsy

A case related to the crown chakra was that of VC, an epileptic woman, aged 25, who was admitted to the Montreal Neurological Institute in 1953, suffering from focal cerebral seizures.[1] The pattern of the seizures consisted of a sense of fear, chills with gooseflesh feelings, amnesia, stiffening, salivation and masticatory movements.

Upon examination, the electroencephalograph (EEG) showed inferior, anterior, mesial temporal, bilaterally independent, predominantly left abnormality. Dr. Penfield operated twice to excise the left temporal lobe. He found that there were adhesions over the tip of the left temporal lobe, with abnormalities in the uncus and hippocampus. Five centimeters of the left temporal lobe were removed, including the full extent of the hippocampus of approximately eight centimeters.

The patient showed definite improvement after the operation and did not develop aphasia, but because of the abnormality of the electrical discharge in the right

---

1. SK did not write up this case formally with medical history, tables of the characteristics of the chakras, etc., as was done with the other cases in the appendix.—ED.

temporal lobe region, the prognosis was guarded. The patient described herself as "pretty impossible, with a terrible temper, the terror of the neighborhood." She was self-centered, impulsive, a poor judge of people, and unable to accept responsibility.

DVK saw the patient in November, 1959, and reported that the color of the general etheric body was bluish-gray, with slight variations around the head and throat areas. There was a small amount of droopiness around the shoulders, more on the right than the left. The movement was on the whole rhythmic and symmetrical except around the head and solar plexus regions, where there was abnormality. In the middle of the head there was a crisscross energy pattern, which is a definite deviation from the norm.

The etheric crown chakra was definitely abnormal in form, size, movement and elasticity. It was unusual in being fine in texture as well as loose, both in the core and in the petals. The color of the petals was golden-blue with a very slight pinkish tinge, which is unusual in this center. The core was bluish-yellow. The brightness was average, but the movement in both core and petals was dysrhythmic, rather slow and variable in speed. The elasticity was variable. The most striking feature was that the petals pointed down. Near the area of three o'clock, some of the petals were out of order and seemed slightly blocked in their energy flow. There was imbalance in the parietal and temporal areas of the left side of the head, and the flow of etheric energy was disturbed. (DVK indicated this by pointing to these regions on the model.)

Because of the unusually close linkage between the etheric and astral fields in the head, when the patient's frequent fits of being overemotional exerted pressure on her etheric energy and diminished its flow to the head, giving her a feeling of "blankness."

Some of her symptoms, and especially the tension she experienced, were related to the astral field. She held grudges, and a state of emotional excitation would trigger a disturbance in the etheric brain, which already had several abnormalities. The crown chakra was definitely abnormal in the petals which were associated with her illness; these abnormalities were related to her emotions and to her loss of consciousness.

The etheric brow chakra was reddish-pink with some yellow and green, in both the core and petals. It was average in luminosity, rhythmic in movement, but below average in speed. The size and form were normal but in places bent slightly down. The elasticity of the core was below average, but the petals were normal. The texture was both fine and loose. The function of the center was moderately normal, but rather dim.

The pituitary gland seemed to be "tight." The etheric energy pattern from the front of the forehead to the center of the brain was dimmer and slower than normal.

In the etheric throat chakra the petals showed considerable pale gray. The brightness was average in the petals but below average in the core. The movement was rhythmic, with low average speed. The form and size were within normal range, but the core was not very sharp and distinct. Although there was no definite leakage in the core, it showed some "wobbling" in the posterior part near the spine. The elasticity was normal, and the texture was both fine and loose. The function of the center pointed to variations in the patterns of the colors associated with its astral counterpart.

The thyroid gland fluctuated in function between hyper- and hypoactivity. The patient had a tendency to easy fatigue.

The etheric solar plexus chakra's core was a darker shade of red compared to the petals, which were reddish-pink. The brightness was below average. The movement was dysrhythmic in both core and petals. The speed of movement was variable, with a tendency to slowness. The size was within normal range, but the core was not sharp and there was some leakage of the energy. The elasticity was better in the core than in the petals. The texture of both parts was at once fine and loose. The function of this center indicated overemotional reactions evidenced by the predominance of red. The absence of sharpness in the core pointed to a tendency toward etheric leakage.

Here again there was an excellent correlation between the subject's medical history and DVK's description of the etheric and emotional patterns.

The Brow Chakra

The Case of CB

Medical History:

1942 - Diabetes Mellitus[1] with Retinitis. Glycosuria was found during pregnancy. Polyuria, Polydipsia and loss of weight. Insulin was given.

1959 - Hypophysectomy (surgical removal of pituitary gland) for therapeutic purposes.

1960 - Received Cortisone, Cytomel and Orinase

Etheric Brow Chakra

Characteristics	*Petals*	*Core*
Color	Gray, red and a little yellow	Duller gray with a few flickering colors
Luminosity	Dull	Dull
Rhythm	Dysrhythmic: slow/ fast pattern	Dysrhythmic: slow/ fast pattern
Rate	Slow	Slow
Size	Normal	Normal
Form	Normal; some down	Not sharp
Elasticity	Poor	Poor
Texture	Coarse and loose	Coarse and loose

Function: Abnormal, very much slowed down.
Pancreas: Granular; the whole physical system is affected.
Liver: Sluggish
Adrenals: Enlarged
Blood Stream: Seems to be affected.
Correlation: Fairly good. The patient looked very sick

---

1. Diabetes Mellitus is a disease associated with certain conditions of the pituitary, thyroid or adrenal glands. The cause is unknown, but in fifty percent of cases there is a history of injury to the head causing damage to the pituitary or a tumor in that area.

and pale. There was some twitching of the face, vomiting and headaches.

The Case of BG

Medical History:

  1953 - Right radical mastectomy for cancer.
  1958 - Decompression of the cord. Laminectomy T1 - T4 Hypophysectomy

Etheric Brow Chakra

Characteristics	Petals	Core
Color	Gray	Darker shade of gray
Luminosity	Dull	Dull
Rhythm	Dysrhythmic	Dysrhythmic: moving in polar opposite to that of pituitary gland
Rate	Slow	Slow
Size	Normal	Normal
Form	Within normal; slightly down	Not sharply defined
Elasticity	Poor	Poor
Texture	Coarse and loose	Coarse and loose

Function: Abnormal by its dysrhythmia, which seemed to affect both sight and hearing. No energy was perceived in the pituitary gland; etherically, it was missing. The etheric brain indicated that the etheric had been affected generally. It was droopy all over the body, including the etheric spine and the back of the neck.

The etheric pancreas showed gray color and dull areas.

Correlation: Excellent. Correlation between the medical status of the pituitary gland and the clairvoyant observations was 100% correct, indicating that the gland was missing. Also, the droopiness along the etheric spine and the back of the neck was correct, for the patient had had laminectomy to the upper thoracic region.

The Case of NS

Medical History:

1949 - Diabetes Insipidus[2]
>   Thirst, polyuria, nervous, jittery, apprehensive, severe headaches in the right occipital-parietal and extending to the forehead, which occurred six months after the birth of a child.

1953 - Hans-Schuller-Christian disease[3] X-ray treatment given for the skull. Osteomylitis of the left ileum which began 14 years previously. A tender lump in left temporal area and right occipital. X-ray showed multiple osteolytic areas in the skull with new lesions appearing. Sella Tursica grossly normal. Patient was given Pitressin 2 units intermuscularly.

1954 - Slight edema of the optic disc.

1956 - Depressions were felt in the skull.

1960 - Disease was in an arrested state. Liver palpable, blood pressure 140/80. Patient was receiving pitressin and phenobarbital.

Etheric Brow Chakra

Characteristics	Petals	Core
Color	Gray	Gray

---

2. Diabetes Insipidus is a chronic disorder of the neuro-hypophyseal system due to a deficiency of casopressin (ADH). All the pathological lesions associated with diabetes insipidus involve the hypothalamic nuclei—the supraoptic and para-ventriculor—or a major portion of the pituitary stalk. One of the causes is posthypophysectomy. The symptoms are excessive excretion of large quantities of very dilute but normal urine and excessive thirst.

3. Half of the patients who have Hans-Schuller-Christian disease develop diabetes insipidus. Some have decreased growth hormone deficiency from the hypothalamic involvement. There is at times a multifocal type of eosinophil granuloma. Patients are usually placed on prednisone and radiation.

Rhythm	Variable dysrhythmia	Dysrhythmic and jerky at point of leakage: 12 o'clock
Rate	Variable; between average and slow	Faster than petals
Size	Normal	Normal
Form	Down	Irregular periphery
Elasticity	Above average	Above average
Texture	Loose and thick	Loose and thick

Function: This chakra is abnormal, as shown by its gray color, irregular core, and leakage at 12 o'clock, and by the looseness and thickness of the etheric material.

Pituitary Gland: The periphery was softer and more stretched out. The center of the gland was more active, and the right side was more active than the left. The pituitary gland seemed to be present.

Skeleton System: The bones on the top of the head in the region of the Fontanelle seemed to be of a thicker type: what DVK called a "bonier bone." The bones seemed harder than in a normal person, and appeared to DVK to be opposite to the bones she observed in the case of Paget's disease (See page 208), in which the bones appeared "crumbly." The elasticity of the bones seemed absent. The bones appeared harder, but not uniformly thick. This increased "boniness" occurred only in patches.

Thyroid Gland: Partially overactive.

Correlation: Excellent. DVK's observations were correct, and corresponded accurately with the medical findings. Her indication that the pituitary gland was present was correct. Her description of the quality of the bones was consistent with medical observations.

The Case of JW

Medical History:

1956 - Diffuse toxic goiter treated with radioactive iodine and Tapazole.

1959 - Left radical mastectomy for carcinoma of the breast with metastases to the lymph glands. Hypophysectomy. Patient was placed on 50 mgm Cortisone daily and Pitressin snuff.
1960 - Basal Metabolism (-24). Patient gaining weight.

Etheric Brow Chakra

Characteristics	*Petals*	*Core*
Color	Gray flecked with green, yellow and red	Gray and darker shade of red
Luminosity	Variable; average to dull with fits of luminosity and dullness	Variable; average to dull
Rhythm	Dysrhythmic	Dysrhythmic
Rate	Average to slow; wobbly movements on right side	Variable; average to slow
Size	Normal	Normal
Form	Abnormal; asymmetrical in size and shape; periphery ill-defined; petals down; right side vague	Abnormal; had no shape; seemed absent
Elasticity	Poor	Poor
Texture	Loose and thick	Loose and thick

Function: This chakra is abnormal by reason of its gray color which indicates decreased energy, by the red which indicates overactivity, and by the speckled colors. Abnormality is also shown by the dysrhythmia, and by its asymetrical shape, and by the periphery, which was so vague DVK could not perceive where it ended.

Pituitary Gland: The center of the gland seemed absent etherically, but the periphery was present and slightly active. The vision was slightly affected.

Correlation: Excellent description of the chakra and of the pituitary gland, which had been excised.

The Throat Chakra

The Case of EB

Medical History:

1953 - Left radical mastectomy for cancer with metastases.

1956 - Hypophysectomy (Surgical excision of pituitary gland). Patient placed on cortisone, pitressin and 62.5 mcg daily. Left hydrothorax.

Etheric Throat Chakra

Characteristics	Petals	Core
Coloı	Gray and blue	Gray and red
Luminosity	Dull	Dull
Rhythm	Dysrhythmic. interrupted pattern	Dysrhythmic: interrupted pattern
Rate	Variable: above average to slow	Variable: average to slow
Size	Normal	Normal
Form	Normal, but down	Irregular periphery
Elasticity	Variable: average to poor	Variable: average to poor
Texture	Fine and coarse	Fine and coarse

Function: The throat chakra is abnormal as shown by the grayness and red color, the irregular periphery, dysrhythmia and a slight indication that the energy in the core was moving in two opposite directions.

Left Breast: The general etheric appears dull and no energy was seen here.

Thyroid Gland: Only part of both the right and left portions of the thyroid was functioning. The upper half of both sides appeared duller when compared to the lower portions of the thyroid. There was also an imbalance in the brightness of the gland.

Legs: The general etheric of the patient's legs was affected.

Correlation: Excellent correlation between the abnormalities observed in this chakra and the medical evidence. The area of the left breast was dull because it had been removed for cancer. DVK's observations relating to the thyroid gland were correct.

The Case of MDL

Medical History:

1941 - Tonsillectomy
Ovarian cyst removed.
1951 - Nodular Goiter, benign, non-toxic, left side larger. Subtotal thyroidectomy (benign adenoma of the thyroid; pathological areas show fibrosis and calcification). Because of hemorrhage, difficulty in breathing developed. Bilateral cord paralysis, which necessitated tracheostomy.
1952 - Hypothyroid and hypoparathyroid symptoms.
1960 - Headaches, dry skin, burning feeling in right leg. Hypoparathyroid uncontrolled.
Patient given Vitamin D, calcium and thyroid extract.

Etheric Throat Chakra

Characteristics	Petals	Core
Color	Gray and blue; edges dull and centers brighter	Gray and red
Luminosity	Average to dull	Average to dull
Rhythm	Dysrhythmic on left side	Dysrhythmic
Rate	Average to slow	Fast to slow
Size	Normal	Normal
Form	Normal, slightly down	Ragged periphery

| Elasticity | Above average | Above average |
| Texture | Coarse and loose | Coarse and loose |

Function: This chakra is abnormal. The red color indicates hyperactivity, and the gray hypoactivity.

Thyroid gland: Indicates that part of it has been removed, and is hypofunctioning.

Parathyroids: These are half-active. DVK believed that at one time they were overactive, but at the time of the examination they were underactive.

Neck: There was extreme tension around the neck, with etheric leakage.

Correlation: Excellent. Observation that part of the thyroid had been removed was correct, also the hyperactivity in spite of the surgery.

The Case of SA

Medical History:

1959 - Mass in neck, easy fatigability. Nodule found in thyroid.

1960 - Bilateral subtotal thyroidectomy.
Increase in weight, cramps in the hands, pulse 60, skin warm, hair smooth. Patient receiving Dexamyl and T3.

Etheric Throat Chakra

Characteristics	Petals	Core
Color	Gray and blue	Darker shade of gray
Luminosity	Dull	Dull
Rhythm	Dysrhythmic, localized to right side	Dysrhythmic, very slow, then quick
Rate	Average to very slow	Average to slow
Size	Normal	Normal

Form	Not normal: down; tiny vortex in one petal moving counterclockwise	Saw-toothed periphery
Elasticity	Poor	Poor
Texture	Coarse and loose	Coarse and loose

Function: This chakra is abnormal.

Thyroid Gland: Flabby; energy level extremely low, as though dead.

Parathyroid: Two of them seemed active, but they were in general hypoactive.

General Etheric: There was an unusual granular, sand-like appearance of the etheric energy distributed over the surface of the whole etheric field, which dipped deep into the physical body as well. This condition was primarily in the legs and neck.

Adrenals: There were spasmodic fluctuations of the etheric energy rhythm, which seemed to be strongly tied to the emotions.

Correlation: Good. DVK's impression was that the patient had strong emotional problems related to sex. Breaks in the astral throat chakra might be the cause of her etheric disturbances. She was the type of patient who would be able to take more thyroid than the average person.

The Case of RS

Medical History:

1948 - Symptoms included pains in various parts of the skull, mainly in the right parietal.

1949 - Paget's disease[1] BMR (plus 36). Tachycardia.

---

1. Paget's Disease (Osteitis Deformances) is a skeletal disease of the elderly, with chronic inflammation of the bones, resulting in thickening as well as softening of the bones, which may become bowed. Its etiology is unknown. The characteristic feature is increased reabsorption of the bone accompanied by an increase

Clinical diagnosis, Hyperthyroid, but no therapy given.

1952 - Increase of hair on face, blurring of vision, pain in upper lumbar region, head enlarged. X-ray showed a questionable calcified shadow of L2 on the right side.

Serum Calcium - 11.5 mgm %

Phosphorus - 2.4 mgm %

Alkaline Phosphotase - 54.6 mgm %

Left hemi-thyroidectomy (lymph adenoma of thyroid)

Left parathyroid remained in place.

Right parathyroid excised for adenoma

1960 - Generalized weakness, pain in bones, right renal calculus, loss of 15 lbs. weight, irregular heartbeat. There was a mass the size of a fist felt in the right lower quadrant, the nature of which was unknown.

Etheric Throat Chakra

Characteristics	Petals	Core
Color	Gray and blue	Gray and red specks
Luminosity	Dull	Dull
Rhythm	Dysrhythmic	Dysrhythmic
Rate	Variable: slow to average	Slow
Size	Normal	Normal
Form	Normal	Periphery ill-defined; fades out
Elasticity	Poor	Poor
Texture	Loose	Loose

Function: This chakra was abnormal. The vortex had slowed down.

---

in bone formation. There are increased levels of the plasma alkaline phosphotases. Urinary stones are common, and at times hypercalcemia is present. Bones affected are the pelvis, femur, skull and vertebrae. There is also a change in the size of the head.

Thyroid Gland: This was "dead-looking" in part; very little was present. Had probably been removed.

Parathyroid Glands: These were not functioning normally; the condition was worse on the right than on the left side. The right side was overfunctioning.

DVK was of the opinion that the patient had a disease of the parathyroids. This was indicated to her by the intensity of the energy in the glands, which seemed to be flickering and out of balance with the energy in the thyroid. Two parathyroids seemed to stand out etherically, with a brighter luminosity radiating out.

Skull: On the right side of the skull near the parietal bone, the bone seemed to be "thinned out." The same characteristics were also found, but to a lesser degree, in the back of the head and in the bones of the spine and legs. The structure of the bones looked "crumbly." In a normal bone the etheric texture looks hard and thick, but in this patient the bones appeared to be in small pieces like bread crumbs. On the right side of the head there was "not enough bone." It did not seem to be complete, and was thin and granular.

The alta major center, which is found in the medulla oblongata, was not functioning properly and acted spasmodically.

Solar Plexus Chakra: An unusual gray color was present in the core of this chakra, which was both dysrhythmic and slow.

Adrenals: These were hypofunctioning, and the liver was slow in function.

Kidneys: The left kidney seemed all right, but there was an indication of a soft stone. The right kidney showed the same "crumbly stuff" in it, and was not functioning normally.

Intestinal Tract: The same "crumbly" material was seen, partially, in the wall of the gut. The function was slow.

Correlation: Excellent, especially observation of the condition of the bones.

The Case of BW

Medical History:

1948 - Fibrous mastitis in left breast.
1952 - Symptoms of hypothyroidism.
1954 - Left thyroid lobectomy for nodular goiter. Pathological report showed a benign goiter with abundant lymphoid infiltration.
1959 - Patient complained of irritability, feeling of cold, fatigue, dryness of skin, loss of curly hair.
1960 - Hypothyroidism, obesity. Patient placed on 75 mcg Cytomel. Later considered to be in a euthyroid state. Basal metabolism -22.

Etheric Throat Chakra

Characteristics	Petals	Core
Color	Gray, blue, orange-red	Gray and red
Luminosity	Average to dull	Average to dull
Rhythm	Dysrhythmic	Dysrhythmic
Rate	Fast	
Size	Normal	Normal
Form	Down	Not sharp
Elasticity	Poor	Poor
Texture	Loose	Loose

Function: This chakra was abnormal.
Thyroid Gland: The center of the etheric thyroid seemed hard and "tight."
Correlation: Excellent.

Here we note that although the thyroid gland was partially excised and the thyroid hormone was below average, which required taking Cytomel, the etheric throat center still showed hyperactivity and abnormality.

The Heart Chakra

The Case of MT

Medical History:

MT, aged 76, had had a very enlarged heart for ten years, with no symptoms of heart failure, no swelling of the feet, no breathlessness. The subject had been very active.

In August, 1985, it was decided to tap the pericardium, from which 300 cc of fluid was aspirated. Although the fluid was clear and the bacteriological tests were negative, the patient was given an anti-inflammatory drug for two weeks. X-rays taken six weeks later showed that the improvement seen immediately after the aspiration from the pericardium remained constant.

On Sept. 27, 1985, DVK observed the patient's heart chakra.

Color -   golden, but with some fluctuation.
Rate -   some dysrhythmia and fluctuation.
Texture - fairly coarse.
Form -   a slight thinning at the periphery of the center.

Looking at the heart and the pericardium, DVK reported that there was a slight heart enlargement, which was normal for the subject. In addition, there was thickening of the pericardial membrane posteriorly, which probably had been present for a long time, and might have been a congenital anomaly. There did not seem to be an inflammatory condition, and there was no evidence of infection.

DVK's impression was that the heart was larger than normal and its pericardial membrane was too tight a fit, and therefore the friction set up between the heart and the membrane during contraction produced the increased amount of fluid in the pericardial cavity. The general vitality of the etheric body was very good.

Correlation: Good. DVK's observation about the lack of an infection or inflammation was verified medically.

The Solar Plexus Chakra

The Case of PT

Medical History:

1930 - Became emotional, cried easily, was suicidal.

1948 - Experienced weakness, poor coordination, numbness, tingling, increased adiposity about the shoulder girdle; increased appetite, easy fatigability. The face became round, and the neck fat, with hypertension, edema of the ankles. Hair began to appear on the face; scalp hair dry and sparse. Diagnosed as Cushing's syndrome.

1950 - Subtotal excision of right adrenal gland. A few months later, left total adrenalectomy was done.

1960 - Patient had improved since operation. Was receiving no medication except when she had an infection and had to take cortisone.

The Solar Plexus Chakra

Characteristics	Petals	Core
Color	Yellow and red	Yellow, red and gray
Luminosity	Average to dull	Average
Rhythm	Markedly dysrhythmic	Markedly dysrhythmic
Rate	Average to slow	Average to slow
Size	Normal	Normal
Form	Normal	Leak
Elasticity	Poor	Poor
Texture	Loose	Loose

Function: This center was abnormal in function. The color gray in the core is unusual, and the great variations in the color of the petals, from dark to pale, as well as in their intensity, indicated there was no uniformity. For example, one petal would be green and orange, and the next petal, although having the same colors, would be either darker or lighter in shade. Similarly, the luminosity showed a great deal of contrast and variability. The dysrhythmia was in the form of a jerk which took place with every turn of the chakra; this condition was present in both the petals and the core. The movement varied from average to slow. The leak in the core appeared on the left side, halfway along its course to the spine.

Adrenals and Pituitary: The left adrenal seemed to have been removed; in DVK's words, "Part of the adrenal is not there." The right adrenal was perceived to be abnormal: the outer part seemed overactive and the inner part underactive.

The energy in the pituitary gland seemed dim. The left ovary seemed dark and its energy was not visible. DVK's overall impression was that the pituitary gland seemed to resemble another case with idiopathic panhypopituitrism. On the whole, the patient seemed balanced endocrinologically because the body had become adjusted to its condition. There was a question as to whether this patient had an unusual type of diabetes.

Correlation: In view of the complexity of the problem, the correlation was fairly good.

The Case of NT

The General Etheric

Color -   Grayish blue, with changes at the solar plexus
Form -   Droopy in the solar plexus area
Texture - Slightly porous and broken at the solar plexus, thick on the chest.

Function: The general function showed an unusual intermeshing between the etheric and emotional energies. There were "open areas" in the emotional body, and at each of these points the etheric appeared thinned out.

These thin places in the etheric field tended to be hypersensitive when the patient was low in energy. This in turn gave rise to many types of fleeting symptoms and/or aches and pains in these areas, none of which appeared to have any organic cause.

DVK described the condition as a "raw spot" which was not being protected from external trauma, and this made the patient susceptible to various neurological symptoms.

The astral body was much involved; it was "open" with gaps, and characterized by a peculiar interaction with the etheric. Although it was brighter than average, its colors were darker, with sweeping movements indicating surges of violent emotion.

Crown chakra: Variable in function. The etheric substance was thicker than normal. There was dysrhythmia over the head, and these variations in movement were probably associated with headaches and a sense of dullness. The energy flow was not constant, leading to tension with periods of low energy.

Pineal and pituitary glands: Not in harmony.

The Brow Chakra

Color -   Thick yellow band alternating with blue and a fainter yellow
Form -   Abnormal on the left side, with leakage

Function: Variable, swinging from plus to minus. The abnormal color pattern indicated that his mental capacity for work was erratic. During mental concentration the golden yellow was strong, but his capacity spasmodic; he tended to tire easily due to the leakage of etheric energy. However, he was capable of a flash of "visual insight," which helped him to see the interrelationships within a problem.

There was an unusual linkage between the emotional and physical bodies; the subject was very sensitive to sound.

Thyroid and adrenals: Did not function together harmoniously.

The Solar Plexus Chakra

Characteristics	Petals	Core
Color	Red, orange	Darker shade of red
Luminosity	Average	Average
Rhythm	Dysrhythmic	Dysrhythmic
Rate	Fast to slow	Fast to slow
Size	Larger than average	Larger than average
Form	Normal	Not sharp
Elasticity	Above average	Above average
Texture	Coarse and loose	Coarse and loose

Function: This center was hyperactive and variable.

The darker shade of red in the core indicated that the subject had very strong feelings which he emphasized. The dysrhythmia may have been induced by his vulnerability to other people's emotions. He tended to become drained of energy via this center. The flow of energy was constantly interrupted, and this in turn affected his digestion. His etheric energy was drained from his solar plexus because of another factor: his close association with a depressed person (his wife). This person literally sucked his energy and slowed down its flow.

His major problem was that he felt other people's emotions to the extent that he was unable to differentiate between his own feelings and theirs. This determined all his reactions to people. The core of the etheric solar plexus became dysrhythmic and interrupted, because it resonated to the rhythm of the people around him. In childhood this had evinced itself by fits of rage, caused by his being overwhelmed by their emotions.

Spleen chakra: The flow of energy via this chakra was variable, as was that from the spleen to the solar plexus. This variable flow interfered with the energy in the stomach, frequently causing digestive problems.

Spine: There were several places in the etheric spine that did not function properly. In about two inches of the central portion (sushumna) the energy seemed to fade out. In some places there was a lighter yellow color, and there were blocked areas where the energy flow seemed swollen and slow moving.

The Spleen Chakra

The Case of LS

History:

The patient was a lecturer and news analyst, who had served as such during World War II and had been considered very reliable and extremely competent. Her predictions about enemy movements were so accurate as to win her distinction. She told us that a map of the battlefront would flash before her eyes, and she would perceive the flags of nations and the direction of their movement. She would then reinterpret the news bulletins in accordance with her visual impressions.

Knowing nothing about the subject or her profession, DVK gave an excellent description of her potential for imagery.

Medical History:

Her main problem was an allergy to certain drugs and a tendency to anaemia.

The Crown Chakra

Characteristics	Petals	Core
Color	Yellow, blue	Brighter blue
Luminosity	Bright	Bright
Rhythm	Rarely dysrhythmic	Rhythmic
Rate	Above average	Above average
Size	Normal	Normal
Form	Normal	Variable, tight or wide
Elasticity	Above average	More elastic than the petals
Texture	Compact, fine	Compact, fine

Function: This center was within normal range. It was very active, and indicated a quick and sensitive mind, with a large capacity for intellectual pursuits. She had a greater ability to concentrate than to meditate, as indicated by the brightness and the presence of blue color.

The Brow Chakra

Characteristics	Petals	Core
Color	Red, yellow, blue	Red, yellow, blue
Luminosity	Above average	Above average
Rhythm	Rhythmic	Slightly dysrhythmic
Rate	Above average	Above average
Size	Normal	Normal
Form	Normal	Normal
Elasticity	Average	Average
Texture	Compact, fine	Compact, fine

Function: This center was normal and active. She had an excellent ability for visualization, as well as psychic sensitivity. She would have flashes of sight, or clairvoyance, but this was not experienced steadily or consistently. (This observation verified by the subject.)

Pituitary Gland: Normal. There was some relationship between it and the thyroid.

The Throat Chakra

Characteristics	Petals	Core
Color	Silvery blue	Silvery blue
Luminosity	Above average	Above average
Rhythm	Variable	Variable
Rate	Average	Above average, but variable
Size	Normal	Normal
Form	Normal	Very slight leakage
Elasticity	Above average	Above average
Texture	Compact, fine	Compact, fine

Function: This center was normal.

Thyroid Gland: Variable in function and might be hyperactive at times, making her tense. "Things go too fast with her."

The Heart Chakra

Characteristics	Petals	Core
Color	Yellow	Really gold
Luminosity	Above average	Above average
Rhythm	Rhythmic	Slight dysrhythmia (Fast/slow)
Rate	Average	Average
Size	Normal	Normal
Form	Slightly larger	Normal
Elasticity	Average	Average
Texture	Compact, fine	Compact, fine

The Solar Plexus Chakra

Characteristics	Petals	Core
Color	Rosy red	Rose, yellow
Luminosity	Above average	Above average
Rhythm	Variable	Dysrhythmic
Rate	Average to slow	Fast
Size	Larger than average, fluctuating in shape	Wider than average
Form	Normal	Wider than average, slight leakage
Elasticity	Above average	Above average
Texture	Compact	Compact

Function: This was the primary center for her psychic sensitivity. She used this center at will when she wished to respond to people in terms of feeling quality. Through it she was able to meet many emergencies.

There was a tendency to digestive disturbance because of this sensitivity.

Correlation: The subject confirmed the sensitivity and the digestive problem.

The Spleen Chakra

Characteristics	Petals	Core
Color	Rose, red with variations	Reddish yellow
Luminosity	Average	Average
Rhythm	Dysrhythmic	Dysrhythmic
Rate	Average	Below average
Size	Normal	Normal
Form	Slightly down	Not sharp, slight leak
Elasticity	Low average	Low average
Texture	Compact, fine	Compact, fine

Function: This center was slightly deviated from normal. There were variations in the colors of the petals, and when they paled this indicated fluctuations in vitality. At these times she did not get enough etheric energy.

The channels of the etheric body between this chakra and the etheric solar plexus chakra were variable, seemingly thin in places, and this affected vitality, blood formation and kidney function.

This center was slower in its function as compared with the other etheric chakras.

Consciousness

The Case of PCK: Schizophrenia

The Etheric Crown Chakra

Characteristics	Petals	Core
Color	Gray and blue	Dark gray
Luminosity	Dull	Dull
Rhythm	Dysrhythmic	Dysrhythmic
Rate	Average to slow	Slow
Size	Smaller than average	Smaller than average
Form	Abnormal: Periphery saw-toothed, droopy	Not sharp: split anterior/posterior
Elasticity	Poor	Poor
Texture	Coarse and loose	Coarse, loose

Function: This center is abnormal. The gray color and gray clouds around the center give a feeling of depression, and their presence in both petals and core indicate the patient is blocked from his higher self. There is a severe abnormality in the core, and a split is seen throughout the center from the anterior to posterior position. Probably a slight leakage is present in the core, which is not sharply defined.

Pineal Gland: Not functioning well. There were no connections with the pituitary gland.

Thalamus: There were irregular impulses in the transmission of etheric energy which sometimes delayed the rhythm.

The Etheric Brow Chakra

Characteristics	Petals	Core
Color	Gray, red and green	Gray and red
Luminosity	Dull	Dull
Rhythm	Dysrhythmic	Dysrhythmic

Rate	Average to slow	Average to slow
Size	Normal	Normal
Form	Abnormal, periphery ragged; peculiar bands of normalcy in between; patches of gray; petals down	Split anterior/posterior, with ragged edges; some leakage
Elasticity	Poor	Poor
Texture	Coarse and loose	Coarse, loose

Function: Abnormal, as shown by the peculiar bands interposed between the normal areas. The gray patches are not healthy, and the split in the center in an anterior/posterior position is also abnormal.

The perception is affected. The ability to visualize, and the rhythm as well as the thalamus seem to be affected.

The Etheric Throat Chakra

Characteristics	*Petals*	*Core*
Color	Blue and gray	Dark blue, almost black
Luminosity	Dull	Dull
Rhythm	Dysrhythmic	Dysrhythmic
Rate	Average to slow	Average to slow
Size	Normal	Normal
Form	Down	Not sharp; leakage at 6 o'clock
Elasticity	Poor	Poor
Texture	Coarse, loose	Coarse, loose

Function: Deviated from normal. The dark blue, almost black core indicates a block from the higher self.
Thyroid Gland: Variable in function.

The Etheric Solar Plexus Chakra

Characteristics	*Petals*	*Core*
Color	Yellow, gray, red	Red
Luminosity	Very dull	Very dull

Function: The red color indicates anger; his emotions took over and tended to function from this chakra. There was a transfer of the seat of consciousness from the head to the solar plexus. The gray color indicates malfunction.

The Case of VPN

Etheric Crown Chakra

Characteristics	Petals	Core
Color	Yellow blue	Gold and blue
Luminosity	Above average	Above average
Rhythm	Normal	Normal
Rate	Above average	Above average
Size	Larger than average	Larger than average
Form	Straight	Sharp
Elasticity	Above average	Above average
Texture	Compact, firm, fine	Compact, firm, fine

Function: This center is normal. The yellow color indicated an exceptional ability to visualize. There was an interconnection between the crown and brow chakras.

Pineal Gland: Functioned above average, and was being stimulated by the flow of energy transmitted from the crown center. Dark blue and royal blue were observed in the pineal gland, indicating that a great deal of etheric energy was moving in and out of this gland. The pineal itself was larger and more active than usual.

Etheric Brow Chakra

Characteristics	Petals	Core
Color	Yellow, red	Orangy yellow
Luminosity	High average	High average
Rhythm	Rhythmic	Rhythmic
Rate	Above average	Above average
Size	Larger than average	Larger than average

Form	Normal, straight	Normal, sharp
Elasticity	Above average	Above average
Texture	Compact, firm	Compact, firm

Function: This center was normal. The yellow color indicated exceptional ability to visualize and concentrate mentally. There was an interconnection between the core of the brow chakra and the pineal gland. The chakra also indicated that the subject had regularly done a great deal of meditating. Everything with regard to this center was very harmonious, and showed a sensitivity which was used in creative work. The subject had a great deal of self-discipline and concentration, as shown by the firmness of the center. The exceptional brightness of the yellow color indicated a capacity to expand consciousness. The interconnectedness and degree of harmony between the crown and brow centers indicated telepathic ability.

Pituitary Gland: This gland was tight and steady in its function.

Etheric Throat Chakra

Characteristics	*Petals*	*Core*
Color	Silvery blue	Darker violet blue
Luminosity	Above average	Above average
Rhythm	Variable	Rhythmic
Rate	Average to slow	Fast to slow
Size	Normal	Normal
Form	Slightly down	Tiny leak
Elasticity	Above average	Above average
Texture	Fine, slightly loose	Fine

Function: Fluctuations in color indicated a disturbance of function. The slight leak showed a deviation from the normal and a point of weakness in the physical body. She used a great deal of energy through her voice when talking with people or speaking publicly. People who drain others tended to pull energy out of her throat center.

Medical correlation: In 1976, following severe bleeding of the stomach which required partial excision of the stomach and duodenum, a temporary swelling of the left lobe of the thyroid became apparent. When health was restored the swelling disappeared.

Thyroid Gland: Fluctuated in its function, and its level of etheric energy was variable.

Etheric Heart Chakra

Characteristics	Petals	Core
Color	Yellow gold	Yellow gold
Luminosity	Above average	Above average
Rhythm	Normal	Normal
Rate	Above average	Above average
Size	Average	Average
Form	Curved upward	Normal
Elasticity	Average	Above average
Texture	Fine	Fine

Function: This center was normal. There was evidence that the physical heart had not been functioning perfectly in the past. This was related to circulation. If the thyroid were improved physiologically, this would help the heart problem. The luminosity and color indicated the subject had long been meditating. Some relationship existed between the throat and heart centers.

Medical Correlation: The subject occasionally had tachycardia.

Etheric Solar Plexus Chakra

Characteristics	Petals	Core
Color	Yellow, red, green	Dark orange, red
Luminosity	Above average	Above average
Rhythm	Normal	Normal
Rate	Variable, average	Fast to average
Size	Above average	Above average
Form	Slightly down	Normal
Elasticity	Below average	Below average
Texture	Fine	Fine

Function: The slight deviation from normal was indicated by fluctuations in the movement and the colors, which varied from pale to darker shades. The digestive system had been affected throughout her life, with poor digestion of fats.

Medical correlation: Correct. In 1976, surgical excision of the stomach was required, as noted above.

Etheric Root Chakra

Characteristics	Petals	Core
Color	Orange, gold	Gold
Luminosity	Above average	Above average
Rhythm	Rhythmic	Rhythmic
Rate	Above average	Average
Size	Normal	Normal
Form	Normal, straight	Normal, sharp
Elasticity	Average	Average
Texture	Compact	Compact

Function: The function was normal, above average in development as indicated by its brightness and activity, indicating that the subject had been meditating.

Adrenal Glands: Good on the whole, but they were being pushed to their maximum capacity of function.

Astral Body

No disturbances were found in the astral body. She had progressed from controlling her emotions to being "detached." Therefore, no real emotional problems were perceived, only those minor and momentary disturbances which everyone experiences. A great emotional shock had taken place six or seven years previously but this seemed to have passed away; there was now no emotional involvement of any kind.

Correlation: Correct. The subject had a very short and happy marriage; the husband died after an illness of several months' duration.

Mental Body

This was larger and brighter than is usual. She had a good telepathic contact with the life around her, as well as communication and inflow from the higher or causal level. This quality was less a feeling than a "knowing," that is, it was not an impression received through the solar plexus but an intuition from the buddhic level.

Healers

The Case of JS

JS was a physician who discovered in his youth that when he touched a person in pain or physical distress his hands would become warm and have a soothing and comforting effect. He used this ability to comfort his child when she had colic, and also to sense the physical condition of his patients. He was, however, very reticent about discussing his ability.

DVK observed the following:

The General Etheric

Color -	Blue-gray
Luminosity -	Above average
Size -	Larger than average
Form -	Wider on the right side, with slight droopiness near abdomen on the left side
Elasticity -	Above average
Texture -	Fine, but slightly thin around the abdomen

Function: The etheric energy was longer around the fingertips, measuring over eight centimeters, indicating a capacity for healing. The etheric body was more fluidic than average, and around his hands it was much more extensive than in the average person. In addition his whole etheric body was wider and more fluidic than is usual. There was a slight droopiness on the left side around the abdomenal region.

The Crown Chakra

Characteristics	*Petals*	*Core*
Color	Blue-gold	Larger amount of blue and gold
Luminosity	Above average	Average

Rhythm	Rhythmic	Rhythmic
Rate	Fast	Low average
Size	Normal	Normal
Form	Normal	Normal
Elasticity	Above average	Average
Texture	Fine	Fine

Function: The chakra was within normal range. The discrepancy in the rate of movement between the petals and the core indicated that the petals responded more quickly than the core. There was conscious control of his meditation.

The pineal gland was active.

The Brow Chakra

Characteristics	Petals	Core
Color	Green and red	Reddish gold
Luminosity	Above average	Above average
Rhythm	Rhythmic	Rhythmic
Rate	Above average	Above average
Size	Larger than average	Normal
Form	Normal	Normal
Elasticity	Above average	Above average
Texture	Fine	Fine

Function: This chakra was normal. The color indicated that there was no constant ability for clairvoyance, but intuitive feeling was more common. The golden yellow in the core indicated an ability for visualization combined with both rational and reflective thought.

Pituitary Gland: Normal

The Throat Chakra

Characteristics	Petals	Core
Color	Yellow-gold	Yellow-gold
Luminosity	Above average	Above average
Rhythm	Rhythmic	Rhythmic
Rate	Above average	Above average

Size	Slightly larger than average	Slightly larger than average
Form	Normal	Normal
Elasticity	Above average	Above average
Texture	Fine	Fine

Function: The chakra was within normal range, but indicated that he had been meditating. There was a harmony between the etheric crown chakra, the brow and the heart chakras.

Thymus Gland: The etheric energy pattern was uneven.

The Solar Plexus Chakra

Characteristics	Petals	Core
Color	Red and green	Reddish, orange, yellow
Luminosity	Above average	Average
Rhythm	Rhythmic	Rhythmic
Rate	Very fast to slow	Very fast to slow
Size	Larger than average	Larger than average
Form	Normal	Not very sharp
Elasticity	Above average	Above average
Texture	Fine, slightly loose	Fine, slightly loose

Function: This chakra was not quite normal. It was not harmonious in its rate and was not functioning as well as the other centers. This was the center through which his sensitivity to other people worked—his strength and his weakness. When in the presence of emotional people he might have a sense of tightness in this area.

Liver: The liver was not detoxifying enough, and was the source of some of his trouble related to the adrenal glands.

The Case of AM

In the case of the healer AM, DVK was asked to observe her as she was working on a patient who complained of general fatigue.

AM placed her hands on the patient, and shortly thereafter reported a tingling sensation in her body as well as her hands, together with a feeling of heat. The patient did not feel anything at first. The healer soon changed the position of her hands and placed them on the right foot, and within a few minutes the patient reported a tingling sensation and feeling of heat on the right side of her body. The healer reported that her hands felt as though they were going to sleep, but without numbness; they felt alive, tingling and warm.

DVK observed that the sense of heat in this case depended upon the recipient, as it was a balancing process. When the healer placed her hands on the spot where there was a disharmony in the flow of etheric energy, the healer's energy increased in response to the patient's need. This helped to restore the energy balance on both sides of the patient's body. The interaction between the healer and the patient was important.

The Solar Plexus Chakra

Characteristics	Petals	Core
Color	Rose, red, *blue*	Red and blue
Luminosity	Above average	Above average
Rhythm	Rhythmic	Rhythmic
Rate	Fast to average	Fast to average
Size	Larger than average	Larger than average
Form	Normal	Normal
Elasticity	Above average	Above average
Texture	Fine and coarse, slightly loose	Fine and coarse, slightly loose

Function: Blue is unusual in this center. When she is emotionally disturbed the blue color changes to gray, which devitalizes her. Both the looseness and the blue color of the chakra indicate some sensitivity, which basically exhibits itself in a feeling of oneness with others. She is likely to be hit by other people's emotions, devitalizing and disturbing her. The solar plexus center is also her strength, and the one she uses to send help to people. There is some connection between this center and the etheric heart chakra.

The Case of AC

The healer AC first became aware of the sensitivity in his hands when he was able to relieve the pain of a burn in his aunt's hand. He described the feeling in his hands as a "sense of heat, electric currents, or a feeling as though my hands were immersed in hot oil." He has since observed that when he tries to heal he feels as though a cobweb-like material is forming at the tips of his fingers, which he can get rid of by shaking or washing his hands.

DVK was asked to observe this cobweb-like phenomenon, which the healer tried to demonstrate on a subject. She reported that the etheric of AC's hands stretched out during the act of healing, and that there was increased elasticity along the fingertips. As he moved his hands back and forth over the subject, he was collecting "dirty or murky" etheric substance and replacing it with better quality or more vital matter. Shaking cleared the healer's hands of this etheric cobwebby material gathered from the patient.

General Etheric Field

Color -	Hazy purple, misty
Luminosity -	Above average
Rhythm -	Slightly dysrhythmic
Rate -	Faster on the right than the left
Size -	Symmetrical, five centimeters in width
Form -	Longer at the fingertips
Texture -	Firm and fine, thin at local points with breaks
Elasticity -	Average

Function: The tension in the etheric is the most important characteristic of this subject; this may affect any part of the body. The etheric flow is variable over the crown and the solar plexus chakras.

The Crown Chakra

Characteristics	*Petals*	*Core*
Color	Blue-gold	Blue-gold
Luminosity	Above average	Above average
Rhythm	Slight dysrhythmia	Rhythmic
Rate	Above average	Average
Size	Normal	Slightly wider
Form	Small frontal leak	Normal
Elasticity	Average	More elastic
Texture	Compact, fine	Fine, slightly loose

Function: The etheric crown center was slightly developed, which indicated an attempt at meditation. The increased speed as well as the slight dysrhythmia showed efforts to meditate. A slight connection was being established between the crown and brow chakras.

Pineal Gland: The pineal was slightly more active than usual, with a minimum connection between the pineal and pituitary glands on the etheric level. The slight leakage of etheric energy in the frontal petals of the center may on occasion give rise to headaches and a sense of pressure in the area.

The Brow Chakra

Characteristics	*Petals*	*Core*
Color	Gold, blue, slightly pink	Bright blue
Luminosity	Above average	Above average
Rhythm	Slight dysrhythmia	Rhythmic
Rate	Above average	Above average
Size	Average	Average
Form	Normal	Normal
Elasticity	Above average	Above average
Texture	Compact, fine	Compact, fine

Function: The center appeared to be slightly under tension, which in turn produced a slight dysrhythmia. There was also dysrhythmia at the point where the brow is interconnected with the crown chakra.

The Throat Chakra

Characteristics	Petals	Core
Color	Purple-blue, silver	Purple-blue, silver
Luminosity	Above average	Brighter than petals
Rhythm	Rhythmic but variable	Slightly dysrhythmic
Rate	Above average	Low average
Size	Within normal	Slightly wider
Form	Normal	Normal
Elasticity	Average	Low average, tight
Texture	Compact, fine	More compact and fine

Function: The chakra was slightly tighter than the average in the core and uneven in its rhythm and function.

Thyroid: The thyroid gland was slightly hyperactive.

The Solar Plexus Chakra

Characteristics	Petals	Core
Color	Varying from dark pink to pale red - uneven	Darker than petals
Luminosity	Above average	More luminous than petals
Rhythm	Variable	Variable
Rate	Above average	Faster than petals
Size	Normal	Normal
Form	Normal	Not sharp, occasional leaks
Elasticity	Above average	Greater than petals
Texture	Coarse, loose	Coarse, loose

Function: Variable, affecting the digestion. This is the center through which he is most sensitive to other people. It is open at the moment of healing.

Bibliography

Arthur Avalon. *The Serpent Power*. Madras, India: Ganesh & Co., 1958.

Lama Anagarika Govinda. *Foundations of Tibetan Mysticism*. New York: E.P. Dutton, 1960.

Hiroshi Motoyama. *Theories of the Chakras*. Wheaton, IL: Theosophical Publishing House, 1981.

C.W. Leadbeater. *The Chakras*. Wheaton, IL: Theosophical Publishing House, [1927] 1981.

David V. Tansley. *Subtle Body: Essence and Shadow*. New York: Thames and Hudson, 1985.

Index

QUEST BOOKS
are published by
The Theosophical Society in America,
Wheaton, Illinois 60189-0270,
a branch of a world organization
dedicated to the promotion of the unity of
humanity and the encouragement of the study of
religion, philosophy, and science, to the end that
we may better understand ourselves and our place in
the universe. The Society stands for complete
freedom of individual search and belief.
In the Classics Series well-known
theosophical works are made
available in popular editions.
For more information
write or call.
1-312-668-1571

We publish books on:
Health and Healing • Eastern Mysticism
Philosophy • Reincarnation • Religion
Science • Transpersonal Psychology
Yoga and Meditation

Other books of possible interest include:

The Astral Body *by Arthur E. Powell*
In-depth study of our emotional, subtle body.

The Chakras *by Charles W. Leadbeater*
Classic look at our body's force center. 10 color illus.

Etheric Body of Man *by Phoebe & Laurence Bendit*
Study of our aura by a psychiatrist and clairvoyant.

The Etheric Double *by Arthur E. Powell*
What is the health aura and what does it do.

Healers and the Healing Process *edited by George Meek*
Case histories of psychic, spiritual and mental healing.

Imagineering for Health *by Serge King*
Self-healing through use of the mind.

Living the Therapeutic Touch *by Dolores Krieger*
Pioneer of this technique describes healing lifestyle.

Spiritual Aspects of the Healing Arts *compiled by Dora Kunz*
Body, mind and spirit as interdependent factors in healing.

Theories of the Chakras *by Hiroshi Motoyama*
An investigation of the force centers in our body.

Available from:
The Theosophical Publishing House
P.O. Box 270, Wheaton, Illinois 60189-0270

"THE CHAKRA SYSTEM"
from
*The Chakras and the
Human Energy Fields*
by
Shafica Karagulla, MD
& Dora van Gelder Kunz
published by
Theosophical Publishing House
POB 270
Wheaton, IL 60189-0270
Phone (312) 665-0123
© 1989 by Dora van Gelder Kunz
ISBN 0-8356-0641-4